DEMYSTIFYING ESPORTS

DEMYSTIFYING ESPORTS

✕ ▢ △ ○

A PERSONAL GUIDE TO
THE HISTORY & FUTURE
OF COMPETITIVE GAMING

BARO HYUN, PhD

COPYRIGHT © 2020 BARO HYUN
All rights reserved.

DEMYSTIFYING ESPORTS
A Personal Guide to the History and Future of Competitive Gaming

ISBN 978-1-5445-1648-6 *Hardcover*
      978-1-5445-1647-9 *Paperback*
      978-1-5445-1646-2 *Ebook*

*For Mir and Haru, my ultimate joy
and our future.*

CONTENTS

INTRODUCTION 9
1. PRESENT-DAY ESPORTS 25
2. THE BACKGROUND 41
3. THE ONLINE GAMING BOOM 55
4. KARAOKE? NO, PC BANGS 71
5. ESPORTS ON CABLE 83
6. GOING PROFESSIONAL 97
7. THE RENAISSANCE OF SOUTH KOREAN ESPORTS 115
8. A PARTY POOPER 133
9. SOCIETAL INTEGRATION 147
    CONCLUSION 165
    REFERENCES 175
    HOW TO CONTACT THE AUTHOR 177
    ACKNOWLEDGMENTS 179
    ABOUT THE AUTHOR 183

INTRODUCTION

An angry grandmother.

That's the reason why I am writing this book.

Here is the story of how one enraged elderly woman inspired me to set down a history of esports, with a view to bridging a gap between generations.

One day I bought two Nintendo Switches as birthday presents for my two sons, who recently turned eight and six, respectively. From the moment the consoles arrived in our house, their grandmother, who supervises their daily activities, entered a state of extreme vigilance.

I've known Yoko for more than a decade. In most circumstances, she is an extremely peaceful person. I've never known her to get mad for no reason. When she sees her grandchildren playing video games, however, a red mist descends over her eyes.

Despite occasional complaints, my older son, Mir, a law-abiding citizen who is more civilized than his brother, seemed to cope with his grandmother's "homework first" doctrine. My younger son, Haru, however, is slightly rebellious and doesn't yet attend primary school—meaning he doesn't have any homework.

When Haru entered gaming mode, he was not at all interested in listening to his grandmother. When she tried to intervene in the middle of his intense engagement with the Switch, he ignored her completely. Sometimes he even retorted by saying something obnoxious ("a six-year-old just said what?!") that he had learned from a YouTube video.

His otherwise peaceful grandmother, on the other hand, couldn't stand the sight of her grandchild giving all his attention to the tiny screen of the Switch for hours at a time, and none to her.

Over the course of a few days, stress in the house gradually built up, until the clouds broke in dramatic fashion.

My sons' granny had a bad day. When she saw the younger one in gaming mode, she flipped out.

With a speed that belied her age, she brought a pair of scissors from the kitchen and mercilessly cut the charging cable of the Switch. Without a cable to charge the machine, my younger son had no way to prolong his gaming when the battery was empty.

His grandmother was victorious yet slightly abashed. My younger son reacted with shock and horror.

HOW MANY ADULTS PERCEIVE VIDEO GAMES

What does the story above tell us? I'd argue that it's a fairly good illustration of how many people in our society perceive gaming. While many young people love to play video games, their older counterparts, especially those who haven't had the chance to experience gaming for themselves, often respond with suspicion, or even outright hostility.

There is a stark gap between people in their thirties, forties, and younger, myself included, who have embraced video gaming as part of their culture, and older generations with little or no gaming experience, who may see video gaming as an alien phenomenon. For many of them, their interactions with video games consist solely of seeing their younger relatives apparently buried in another world, unable to socialize or pay attention to events off the screen. They naturally form a negative perception of gaming that can be hard to shake.

Esports is everywhere nowadays, so these same older people are sure to hear about it on the news. They don't fully understand what esports is and—based on their limited interactions with video games—they think negatively about it.

It's an entirely understandable situation, but I think it's an extremely unfortunate one. This generation gap is felt by parents of children who love games and children whose parents *don't* love games. Worse, it's a worldwide phenomenon. I have seen many people facing the same issue in Japan—where I currently live—the United States, and Europe, where I have previously lived.

The good news is that there's no need for esports to drive a wedge between generations when they could instead be a point of intergenerational connection.

That's why I wrote this book. As a parent of two children who love video games, I can see the risks of excessive gaming. Yet as an esports enthusiast myself, I understand *why* my sons enjoy them so much. I hope I can be a bridge between the generation of digital natives who feel completely at home in the world of esports and an older generation of people who feel perplexed, even threatened, by the virtual worlds their relatives inhabit.

If you have limited experience playing games but your children or grandchildren are avid gamers, this book is for you. Perhaps you already feel negative toward video games in general and you want to understand why so many younger people love them. The gaming industry isn't perfect. It has focused too much on creating entertainment, leading to a perception of video games as a guilty pleasure. But there are numerous positive elements of video gaming.

This book is about the history of competitive gaming, now called esports. In these pages, I describe how esports took off as a subculture, how it formed into an industry, and how it mushroomed into a global phenomenon. If you are curious to know more about the history, so you can understand younger members of your family who are heavily into competitive gaming, you'll find ample insight in this book.

Alternatively, perhaps you've seen so much about esports in the media that you want to familiarize yourself with it. Even if you don't have a personal connection with an esports fan, reading this book will provide you with a history of the esports industry and an understanding of the new career paths it has opened up to members of younger generations.

Let's acknowledge another possibility. Perhaps you're a young person who is serious about gaming. You aim to carve out a career for yourself in the esports industry, but you still haven't figured out how to explain your ambition to your parents. If your parents are highly conservative, you may wonder how you could ever explain to them what esports mean to you.

Or maybe you simply want to understand the history and business of an industry that brings you a lot of pleasure. How did esports start and how do they differ from standard video gaming?

When communication breaks down, we all lose. If you're a parent, you may resort to premature judgments about your child's life and career choices, for example, believing that he is hopeless because he spends too many hours every day playing games, or that he is nuts for wanting to become a professional gamer. On the other side of the coin, if you're a young person with an avid interest in esports, you may think your parents are clueless.

The only way to bridge this gap is by making a conscious effort to understand the perspectives of the important people in your life. I hope this book will represent the first step in that effort.

MY ESPORTS STORY

You may be wondering what gives me the authority to write about esports. When it comes to gaming, I have roughly an average amount of experience for my generation. Although I spent a moderate amount of time gaming during my childhood and teenage years, I am no professional gamer. Nonetheless, like any other Korean male of my generation, I enjoy watching professional gamers play competitively.

My first game console was a Nintendo that my parents bought me when we lived in Pittsburgh, Pennsylvania. I was five or six years old. The next landmark I remember is moving to Seoul, South Korea, where I owned a series of video game consoles, such as a Super Nintendo and a Sony PlayStation.

Around the time I entered a local junior high school, PC games became more popular than console games in South Korea. Throughout my time living in Seoul, as a high schooler and as a college student, the heat never went out of gaming. Enthusiasm for competitive gaming only grew. Years later, the world would dub this phenomenon "esports."

While I was training as an aerospace engineer, and during my career in the research and development department of a major Korean automaker, video games were an occasional hobby but nothing more.

Years later, I switched my career path to business management consulting and joined a Big Four consulting firm based in Tokyo, Japan, where I currently live. Growing up as a big fan of Japanese video games and watching the esports scene grow globally, I expected that Japan would have a decent-sized esports market, at least matching South Korea or the United States.

But to my great surprise, when I joined the firm in 2017, the term "esports" was still foreign to the majority of the Japanese people.

This observation soon evolved into a realization that the relative dearth of esports in Japan might be a good business opportunity. Japan has one of the largest video gaming industries in the world, surely ripe for esports development. I started to work on establishing an esports business practice at a consulting firm traditionally known for its auditing, accounting, and risk management service, not subject areas remotely related to esports.

At first, nobody in the firm understood what I was trying to do. But after about a year of internal seminars, pitches, and discussions, the firm agreed to launch an esports advisory group, which I currently lead. We sent out our first official press release in May 2018. To the best of my knowledge, we were the first member of the Big Four to launch such a service, not only within Japan but also globally. I am very grateful for this.

Now, about two years since the launch of the new practice, what began as a side project has become my main focus as the number of clients, along with the number of people in my team, has grown steadily. Over the course of those two years, I came to realize that this may be my calling.

Many of my clients, most of whose businesses are superficially unrelated to gaming, want to incubate a new service aimed at the growing esports industry. My team helps them understand the market. As a part of our advisory service, we often provide them with an overview of the market, both quantitative and qualitative. For me, the intersection is perfect. My esports experience from South Korea has served me and my clients very well and formed the basis of our esports practice.

WHY AIM THIS BOOK AT PARENTS?

With my business interest in esports, you may wonder why I am aiming this book at individual parents instead of targeting potential clients. The reason is that I believe there is a bigger story to be told about the history of esports in South Korea.

I have seen many potential esports clients turn down attractive business proposals. Why? Not due to a lack of prospects in the field, but because key decision-makers were ignorant of the subject. On many occasions, I have spent weeks in collaboration with a client, preparing a business pitch for a new esports project, only for a senior executive who didn't seem to fully understand the subject to exercise a veto. It's a frustrating experience.

I had what I thought was a business problem. In response to this, I initially wanted to write a primer on esports business. In every industry, I talk to executives who seem to like esports' market prospects. They consume reports and articles about competitive gaming, but they seem to hit a wall and don't look further. I wanted to find a way of reaching executives, something more compelling than a blunt business proposal. That something was going to be this book.

I realized that, growing up in South Korea, for so long the epicenter of a thriving esports scene, I have a wealth of personal stories on the subject. Yet I couldn't find any books that dived in to the story of esports in South Korea in the depth I knew I could. The stories I want to tell have both business and personal value. In a business context, they help clients to qualitatively understand the present-day esports business and its prospects. The more potential clients understand the prospects, the more excited they are to work with me in my capacity as an esports advisor. "Great," I thought. "I'll write a book explaining how esports can solve my clients' business problems."

As I pondered this idea, I reached an epiphany. I might be able to solve a business problem, but—as you'll see—the esports industry faces bigger problems. It is beset not only by the ignorance of individual businesspeople, but by a subtle stigma around video gaming from a generation who never had the chance to embrace esports. "At their core," I thought, "don't many people still perceive video gaming negatively? Isn't that the real problem I want to address?" And then Yoko cut the charging cable of my son's Nintendo Switch, and an abstract problem came into sharp focus. Suddenly, the book I was writing to solve my clients' business problems grew into a book that can address a universal generational problem.

Esports in South Korea has a fascinating history. When I was a gaming kid in the nineties, the social perception of video gaming was extremely negative. Two decades later, that perception has evolved to the point where South Korea has embraced esports as a part of the culture. If that can happen in South Korea, surely it can happen anywhere. I discovered that I wanted to share the story.

Business goals aside, therefore, I hope this book will also prove educational. I aim to interweave my personal stories with historical facts, describing that transformative time in South Korea and giving readers a firsthand insight into video gaming subculture. I believe the stories in these pages have the power to shift the negative connotations many parents still hold regarding video games to positive connotations. These parents may have little experience of video games. They may not be business-minded. But they live with game-loving children and seek educational resources because they want to understand the phenomena that capture their children's attention.

As a result of this educational ambition, I may be casting a wider net than I need to reach my core business audience. If so, I'm okay with that. The better laypeople understand esports, the more business prospects the industry may expect in the future.

Finally, history moves fast. Do today's esports enthusiasts know how the scene took off in South Korea? Probably not, at least not in the detail described in this book. I hope this book can be a resource for anyone—parent, businessperson, or avid gamer—who wants to understand that history.

WHAT YOU'LL FIND IN THIS BOOK (AND WHAT YOU WON'T)

This book is a broad historical survey of the development of esports, from a personal perspective. In it, you'll find a collection of stories, backed by some facts and business insights acquired during my time as a business management consultant, that are relevant to your understanding of esports.

I don't pretend to be wholly objective, and this book is not intended to be a comprehensive research paper on esports or a business handbook. I cannot determine the value of esports for you, but I can share with you the history of how it developed in South Korea, backed by personal anecdotes from my time as a teenage boy discovering esports.

Esports sometimes seems like an incredible mystery. As you'll see, it doesn't need to be. Specifically, you will learn about:

- The historical foundation of esports in South Korea
- The esports business ecosystem
- The types of careers within the esports industry
- The exciting esports renaissance in South Korea
- How the esports bubble—like other bubbles—is vulnerable to popping
- What Korean society looks like after two decades of esports
- The most popular genres of esports games
- Why people enjoy watching competitive gaming
- Why professional players are smart, intelligent, and dedicated

You may never be able to beat your kid at their favorite video game, but after reading this book, you will be a lot more knowledgeable in the history and business of esports. You may even be able to teach your kid a thing or two about career paths, risks, and growth.

It's important to acknowledge that the esports scene is extremely game-specific. Different genres and titles attract completely different cross-sections of society. This book is biased toward a specific game called *StarCraft*, which played a critical role in establishing the Korean esports scene. I will explain more about *StarCraft* in the following chapters.

I also want to acknowledge that, while I have done my best to straighten out supporting facts, some parts of this history may not be detailed enough for some readers. This is because I have tried to produce a cohesive story, as opposed to a comprehensive history. I want this book to be accessible to the layperson seeking a leisurely read on a commute to work, a toilet break, or a lazy afternoon at a cafe.

Finally, allow me to explain why so much of this book is focused on South Korea. The simple reason is that South Korea is the nation you need to know in order to understand esports. It is the birthplace of the esports business. Even though it never had a huge gaming market, it has proven uniquely fertile ground for esports.

To deeply understand the fundamentals of what is happening at present on a global scale, I claim that it is critical to understand how the ecosystem was formed in the birthplace of esports over two decades ago. When you bear this foundation in mind, you will find it easier to comprehend what is happening in the present-day esports scene, even if you don't have a great deal of experience with gaming or video game technology.

To understand the cosmos, astrophysicists study the

Big Bang theory (not the American TV hit but the actual theory); likewise, to understand esports, we study the birthplace of esports.

Are you ready to demystify esports? Then keep reading.

CHAPTER 1

PRESENT-DAY ESPORTS

What does a typical esports gamer look like?

At home, we are talking about a personal gamer, locked in his or her room in front of a gaming PC, playing first-person shooters for hours. These shooting games take place in a crowded virtual battlefield, with many other gamers simultaneously connected online. These other gamers come from around the globe, as near as the neighboring house, as far away as the other side of the world.

The typical gamer plays using a headset, talking constantly to teammates to exchange information about opponents and develop strategies. The atmosphere is intense, so sometimes—if not most of the time—the language is littered with swear words, especially when things aren't going well.

Expanding our view outwards, the heart of the esports scene lies in tournament competition. This is when the gaming world moves out of the bedroom and into the stadium. Tens of thousands of people gather in sports arenas to watch teams of professional gamers playing against each other on stage, surrounded by shiny neon lights and complete with team jerseys. The atmosphere rivals an NBA match or the concert of a hip rock star.

Interestingly, unlike sporting events and live concerts, where the physically interesting stuff happens directly in front of the audience, the core appeal of esports events is a game taking place in a virtual space—an online video game.

Professional video gamers are as highly motivated as professional sportspeople, and as determined to win. There is a lot at stake for them, for example, the glory of victory, the vindication of years of hard practice, recognition by the global game community, opportunities for new sponsorship deals, and of course hefty prize money, often millions of dollars. The total pool of prize money at esports events in 2019 was more than $211 million.[1] The largest prize pool for a single event was a major tournament event for a game called *Dota 2*, known as The International 2019. The prize pool for The International topped $34 million.

---

1   Kevin Hitt, "The Top 10 Esports of 2019 by Total Prize Pool," *Esports Observer*, December 27, 2019, https://esportsobserver.com/biggest-esports-2019-prize-pool/#:~:text=2019%20was%20an%20incredible%20year,Records%20were%20set%20in%202019.

Some spectators at esports events don't bother watching the giant screens installed at the venue. They prefer to follow the action more privately, for example, through their smartphones. Online live streaming services such as YouTube and Twitch are attracting so many viewers that audience numbers have already surpassed those recorded for some major sports events. Goldman Sachs, for instance, reports that the 2017 finals of a game called *League of Legends* attracted 58 million viewers, whereas the MLB World Series the same year pulled in 38 million viewers, the NBA Finals 32 million, and the NHL Stanley Cup Finals 11 million.[2]

The earnings of top esports players are astronomical. Up to 2018, a twenty-six-year-old *Dota 2* esports professional named KuroKy had earned more than $4.13 million from ninety-two tournaments, almost as much as the average annual salary of an MLB player—$4.41 million in 2018, according to Statista.

The massive popularity of esports hasn't gone unnoticed by corporate giants. In 2018, McDonald's stopped renewing its fifteen-year sponsorship deal with the German Football Association, the organization that runs four-time World Cup champion and Germany's top-tier professional football

---

[2] Katie Jones, "How the eSports Industry Fares Against Traditional Sports," *Visual Capitalist*, September 3, 2019, https://www.visualcapitalist.com/how-the-esports-industry-fares-against-traditional-sports/.

league, the Bundesliga. In place of that deal, McDonald's chose instead to initiate a deep partnership with ESL, a prominent esports league brand, by signing a decade-long deal.[3]

I hope these snapshots have given you an insight into the magnitude of the esports scene. Now let's explore the market as a whole.

AN ECONOMIC PERSPECTIVE

According to Newzoo, a well-respected esports market research group based in the Netherlands, the global esports market in 2019 generated revenues of $950.6 million, up 22.4 percent year-on-year.[4] In the same year, the global esports audience reached 443 million, reflecting year-on-year growth of 12.3 percent.

This two-digit market growth in the esports market is particularly noteworthy because it comprehensively outstrips the traditional sports market. A report by The Business Research Company predicts that, by 2022, the global tra-

---

3   Richard Welbirg, "McDonald's Quits German Football, Doubles Down on Esports," *SportBusiness Sponsorship*, November 5, 2018, https://sponsorship.sportbusiness.com/news/mcdonalds-quits-german-football-doubles-down-on-esports/.

4   Dean Takahashi, "Newzoo: Global Esports Will Top $1 Billion in 2020, with China as the Top Market," *VentureBeat*, February 25, 2020, https://venturebeat.com/2020/02/25/newzoo-global-esports-will-top-1-billion-in-2020-with-china-as-the-top-market/.

ditional sports market will rise at an annual rate of around 6 percent.[5]

Leaders in the traditional sports industry are concerned that their core fan base is aging, while new fans are not flocking to their sports as rapidly as they would like. In a world of on-demand content services, such as YouTube and Netflix, the traditional television business is losing its power to determine what people watch. As that power wanes, so does traditional television's influence on the sports business.

Imagine that your college-aged son or daughter wants to kill the next couple of hours consuming some content. Nowadays, they have a huge number of options to choose from. Watching an NFL or English Premier League (EPL) match with friends, at home or at a bar, used to be perceived as a "must-do" option. Nowadays, however, young people can watch an on-demand Netflix drama, play a few rounds of online gaming with friends, or simply enjoy a series of random YouTube videos.

With all the other options for consuming content, the odds of choosing traditional sports have been lengthening. In

---

[5] I think even 6 percent is an optimistic figure. As I write this page in March 2020, the globe is seriously hit by the COVID-19 pandemic. As a result, most of the major sports leagues in the world have either been suspended or canceled, and the Tokyo 2020 Olympics have been postponed.

this environment, the two-digit growth of the esports industry is an excellent indication of its popularity.

Where do people actually spend money in the world of esports? The simple answer is that the esports ecosystem is similar to the traditional sports ecosystem. Fans purchase tickets for tournament events, team merchandise (e.g., team jerseys), game-related products, gaming PC-related products (e.g., a good keyboard, mouse, and gaming chair cost a fortune), and other merchandise.

Fans also make donations to people who stream their gaming live, using services such as Twitch or YouTube. Online donation is unique to the esports scene, so allow me to elaborate further. Top esports players practice live in front of a camera and broadcast their sessions. When fans see an awesome piece of gameplay that impresses them, they donate directly to the player using a digital currency. This is different from a pay-to-watch entrance fee, and even from the kind of coerced "donation" that occurs in places like strip clubs, because it's completely voluntary.

Media rights generate a big portion of industry revenue: In 2018, 18 percent of global esports income ($160.7 million), came from media rights.[6] That figure represents a

---

[6] Jurre Pannekeet, "Newzoo: Global Esports Economy Will Reach $905.6 Million in 2018 as Brand Investment Grows by 48%," Newzoo, February 21, 2018, https://newzoo.com/insights/articles/newzoo-global-esports-economy-will-reach-905-6-million-2018-brand-investment-grows-48/.

whopping 72.1 percent year-on-year growth. When viewer numbers are taken into account, this level of growth is hardly surprising.

The *Washington Post* reported that 15 million people watched the 2018 Kentucky Derby, 9.44 million people watched the Wimbledon tennis championship, and 9.1 million viewed the 2018 US Open in golf.[7] In 2017, an esports *League of Legends* championship commanded a peak audience of 106.2 million people, seven times more than the Kentucky Derby. According to technology consulting firm Activate, US esports audiences will likely exceed those of the NFL by 2021.[8]

Unlike traditional sports, esports involve people playing video games, which are proprietary products. Therefore, intellectual property (IP) rights represent another major source of income: in 2018, 13 percent of global esports revenue ($116.3 million) came from game publisher fees, representing a relatively moderate 11 percent year-on-year growth.

Game publishers have ways of monetizing their IP. From

---

[7] Christopher Ingraham, "The Massive Popularity of Esports, in Charts," *Washington Post*, August 27, 2018, https://www.washingtonpost.com/business/2018/08/27/massive-popularity-esports-charts/.

[8] Syracuse Staff, "With Viewership and Revenue Booming, Esports Set to Compete with Traditional Sports," Syracuse University, January 18, 2019, https://onlinebusiness.syr.edu/blog/esports-to-compete-with-traditional-sports/.

a business-to-consumer (B2C) perspective, most games available nowadays are completely free to download and play, a stark change from the days when gamers had to buy software just to play the game. But free game content doesn't necessarily imply that there are no revenue streams. The most popular games are cleverly designed to encourage players to purchase in-game items, for example, outfits that give game characters a unique look.

Some games, such as *League of Legends*, offer a palette of characters for players to select, but only some are available for free. In order to choose the non-free characters, players need to earn virtual game money, either by building their experience in the game or by paying cash.

In most games, paid items don't directly influence the odds of winning the game. But sometimes these items are essential because they provide more strategic options. Some strategy games provide a pool of game maps. Each map may require novel tactics to defeat another player. There may be a bundle of maps that players can freely choose, while the most entertaining ones need to be purchased.

From a business-to-business (B2B) perspective, organizers of esports tournaments need permission from game publishers to use their games. This usually requires an agreement between the organizer and the game publisher, involving a lump-sum fee up front or a percentage of tournament revenue.

IS ESPORTS JUST A BUZZWORD?

You may wonder whether esports is nothing more than a buzzword that has caught the media's attention and is enjoying a moment in the sun.

That's categorically not the case.

Although esports has flown under the radar for many years, it has been more than two decades since the industry took off in South Korea. The media's attention is only a reflection of the growing significance of esports, in terms of market growth and cultural integration.

The Asian Games (also known as Asiad) is a competitive sports event similar to the Olympics, exclusively for Asian and Pacific countries. Asiad has been held every four years since the early 1950s. The organizing committee of Asiad has announced that, beginning at the 2022 Asiad in Hangzhou, China, esports will be an official medal sport. Backing this decision, a pilot esports match took place during the 2018 Asian Games in Indonesia.

The organizing committee of the Olympics is also engaged in early discussions about the inclusion of esports as an official medal sport. Since 2018, the International Olympic Committee (IOC) has opened a series of esports forums. Why on earth would the IOC bother to spend their precious time discussing esports? Some speculate that the sports industry is gradually losing its young fan base and that finding ways to incorporate esports is a possible solution to the issue.

HOW DID VIDEO GAMING BECOME ESPORTS?

The transformation from video gaming to esports was made possible for one simple reason: it's fun to watch people playing video games competitively. Really. That is all.

Watching people who are extremely good at playing video games is a highly saleable product, at least as appealing to gaming fans as content such as YouTube videos, Netflix dramas, and sports matches. This fact is the key driver of the game-to-esports transformation.

If you are good enough at a game, people who care about it will spend precious cash to watch you play competitively. And, counterintuitive as it may seem, these need not necessarily be active gamers themselves. They may not play the game they are following at all. In reality, this is quite similar to sports fans. I may avidly follow the English Premier League (indeed I used to), but I never play soccer myself.

This passive form of engagement is not completely new. Back in the days of game arcades, it wasn't hard to spot spectators gathering around some dudes dueling at *Street Fighter*, *Tekken*, or *Mortal Kombat*. They may not have been professionals, but they were good enough to make watching them entertaining.

If we look even further back, it becomes clear that people have been watching other people play video games for almost half a century. The first esports event was likely held at Stanford University in 1972, using a game called *Spacewar!*[9] Another milestone that is still discussed in the game community is the story of Dennis "Thresh" Fong. Fong won a *Quake* (a popular first-person shooter) tournament in 1997. His prize was a Ferrari, donated as the grand prize by John Carmack, co-founder of a video game company called id Software. Fong is in the *Guinness World Records* for being the first professional gamer.[10]

Passive game engagement attracts broader audiences than active engagement because it has a lower participation threshold. It takes more effort to engage actively with games than to engage passively. For someone to play a video game properly, they need proper hardware (e.g., a

---

9 Roundhill Team, "Esports Viewership vs. Sports in 2019," Roundhill Investments, February 12, 2020, Https://Www.Roundhillinvestments.Com/Blog/Esports-Viewership-Vs-Sports.

10 Dean Takahashi, "Dennis 'Thresh' Fong on Competitive Gaming, Then and Now," *VentureBeat*, April 21, 2018, https://venturebeat.com/2018/04/21/dennis-thresh-fong-on-competitive-gaming-then-and-now/.

game console or a good spec PC) and game software, and they must learn the basic rules of the game, which will take some time. And this is just as an entry-level degree of active engagement. Those who want to be good at a game will need to invest more time and resources.

Passive engagement, on the other hand, requires significantly less effort. All a viewer needs to do is find their favorite channel or event and watch. How hard is watching a YouTube video? This low bar to entry means that there are broader audiences for watching games than for playing them.

For a businessperson, esports fans represent a far greater opportunity than esports competitors. This extension to passive engagement also means that esports involves many stakeholders, creating a larger business ecosystem than the traditional game market. The business ecosystem of the traditional game market relied on active engagement. Therefore, it hinged heavily on the relationship between game publishers and game players. The esports ecosystem is much broader. Stakeholders include tournament event organizers, professional players, professional teams, sponsors, broadcasters, game publishers, and fans.

WHY IS SOUTH KOREA SO IMPORTANT TO ESPORTS?

As the country where the esports business ecosystem was first formed, and where it has been sustained to this day,

South Korea is an essential part of esports history. This may not be well known, even within the present-day esports community. Until now, what has happened in the East has stayed in the East.

Moreover, the South Korean esports market has several interesting characteristics. Namely:

1. The game that incubated esports and launched its popularity in South Korea was created by a foreign (American) company. At the time, Korea had no significant esports game publishers.
2. South Korea responded organically by creating unprecedented esports businesses in response to market needs. These included net cafes, esports-only cable channels, and professional esports teams.
3. The births of these new esports businesses were interrelated. Different types of businesses helped one another, creating a virtuous cycle that generated a sustainable esports ecosystem. For some time during the 2000s, the Korean esports industry was highly prosperous, exercising significant influence on the global esports scene.
4. The Korean esports ecosystem was almost destroyed by misconduct, most notably a match-fixing scandal in 2010 that turned the industry upside down.
5. The esports scene in South Korea has weathered these storms and become a solid subculture, deeply integrated into Korean society.

This is why understanding the growth of esports in South Korea is such an essential part of demystifying the ecosystem as a whole.

In comparison with the United States, Japan, and China, South Korea does not have a large gaming market. But it is the home country of some of the best professional esports players in the world, partly due to the country's developed esports ecosystem. Korean teams, for instance, have won *League of Legends* World Championship titles in multiple consecutive seasons and emerged three-time gold medalists in the *Overwatch* League. The 2019 tournament winner, San Francisco Shock, boasts six Korean players in a ten-person lineup.

A consequence of South Korea's position in the global esports ecosystem is that Koreans have earned an international reputation as fantastic gamers, in the same way as many people assume that Brazilians will be good at soccer. When I was an engineering graduate student in the United States, a Turkish classmate who learned my nationality commented, "You must be very good at *StarCraft*." Call it stereotyping, but this is a reputation South Koreans have earned over time.

Thanks to this developed esports ecosystem, Korea may have the highest public esports literacy in the world. I'm probably on the far-left side of the Korean esports literacy bell curve, but I still know how to play most esports games, follow the professional leagues, and occasionally watch esports matches on YouTube. As a player, I was pretty bad at *StarCraft* in comparison with my friends. Nonetheless, I knew how to play, understood basic strategies such as build orders, and memorized all the keyboard shortcuts. At a friendly social gathering, especially after a drink or two, I have no problem playing a friendly match. When you consider that most of the Korean population is more engaged with esports than I am, you can imagine how knowledgeable and crafty they are.

Naturally, the Korean esports ecosystem did not emerge fully formed overnight. South Korea's transformation into an esports nation happened more slowly and subtly. In the following chapters, I am going to share more detail about the transformation that occurred in South Korea, starting in the nineties. At the time, I was one of many helpless junior high schoolers based in Seoul, frivolously playing games with classmates just like any other teenager.

The stories I will share in upcoming chapters are mostly based upon my personal experiences as an average gaming kid, sprinkled with some business insights that stem from my present-day consulting experience.

The story begins with some social context from South Korea in the nineties.

CHAPTER 2

THE BACKGROUND

In the early nineties, I was an ordinary kid in elementary school in Seoul who loved to play video games. I have two vivid memories of those times: game consoles and arcades. Many of my friends owned a Japanese game console, mostly a Nintendo Entertainment System, Super Nintendo, or Sega Mega Drive.

All these game consoles needed software cartridges that were purchased separately from the machine. Ownership, however, was permanent. There were no subscription options. If a player got bored of a specific title, they could swap the cartridge with friends for other new and interesting titles.

The concept was simple. The act of buying video game cartridges as a kid in Seoul was quite a challenge, however.

Why was this? Where I lived, there were few local game shops. Those that did exist charged premium prices for titles that could be purchased more cheaply elsewhere. As a teenager, I did not have a solid income and paying fifty to eighty dollars per game cartridge was beyond my means.

But there was an alternative solution: a trip to the Yongsan electronics district.

THE LONG AND WINDING ROAD TO YONGSAN

Yongsan is an area in the heart of Seoul that was famous in the mid-nineties as a huge electronics marketplace. With countless game shops, market supply and competition drove the prices of gaming software down to a much more affordable level than buying at a local shop.

For a game-loving teenager, probably the most common way to independently afford a game title was to save up income from scarce sources throughout the year, such as relatives giving out pocket money during holiday seasons, then take a trip to Yongsan to buy coveted titles as cheaply as possible. For gamer kids whose mental universe revolved around video games, Yongsan was the utopia; the mecca; the Garden of Eden. But we adults understand that the road to heaven is never short and straight. So it was with the road to the Yongsan electronics district.

Many gamer kids in Seoul had the same idea to save up money then go shop in Yongsan. Back then, hardly any sane Korean parent supported their children in playing video games, so the teenagers went shopping for games alone or with friends. For some kids, the journey to Yongsan meant taking public transportation and leaving the comfort zone of their local area for the first time in their life. It was like the scene in *Lord of the Rings* where the hobbit Frodo Baggins leaves his hometown of the Shire for the first time, to seek the One Ring.

If the road to Yongsan was winding, it became even more treacherous when it reached Yongsan. A group of elementary schoolers carrying a large sum of money (around one hundred dollars) to spend on video games looked like an extremely good target to some people, namely street-rat teenagers with the physique to overpower them. These street rats were willing and able to take this money by force.

For the street rats, these young Frodos were an easy source of income. Their modus operandi was simple: secretly approach any group of youngsters who arrived in Yongsan looking to purchase video games, guide them to somewhere less visible, using brute force if needed, then demand money and threaten them with violence. If they refused to comply, the street rats warmed up their fists until they became more flexible.

For innocent young Frodos who had traveled all the way

to Yongsan, this was a terrifying experience. Many victims were unable to resist and lost their annual holiday savings in an instant. Where were the police? God knows where, but definitely not in the vicinity of Yongsan.

Soon Yongsan was filled with these teenage gangsters, who hunted down young game shoppers as zealously as hungry hyenas hunt down antelopes in Africa. The area soon earned a double reputation—a gamers' heaven whose gates were guarded by demonic bandits.

Despite the fears and frustrations of venturing into Yongsan and risking losing our money and our pride, we gamers refused to give up on our hobby. We had to be creative. We had to deal with the situation.

I had a friend with whom I always went to Yongsan, a gamer and Japanese culture fanatic. My friend stopped using his usual wallet, knowing it was the first thing the bandits would search for when he encountered them. Instead, he covered his cash in a napkin and placed it underneath the insole of his shoe. The Yongsan demons would check his pocket, some would even look in his shoes, but they never looked underneath the shoe insole.

Another friend started to use spy gadgets, such as an ordinary-looking wallet with a hidden compartment, from where the cash was only accessible through an unusual opening. Some people got even more cunning. They used a decoy strategy, carrying some cash in a normal wallet to surrender when accosted, but keeping most of their money somewhere hidden. The coolest spy wear I saw was a belt with a hidden zippered pocket.

This is how we coped with the harsh environment of Yongsan as young gamers.

SOFTWARE PIRACY

Even if we gamers succeeded in evading the street rats of Yongsan, consoles and game titles consumed most of our money—hundreds of dollars for the consoles and fifty dollars or more for the games. Of course, we gradually got tired of even our favorite games and desired new titles—role-playing games (RPGs), sports games, adventures, action games, simulations, etc.

There was no way normal schoolkids could afford so many games. What to do? Except for those rare fortunate kids whose parents were highly supportive of their video gaming, most young gamers felt they had no option but to turn to the dark side: illegally modifying their games consoles so they could run *pirated software titles that were more affordable*. This was quite easy to do. Consoles could be modified at local game shops for a small fee, and the service was performed quickly.

Imagine playing the same game titles at a fraction of the price of authentic ones. Schoolkids loved this solution. It was a salvation for many gamers.[1] Some people warned that unprofessional modification could shorten the life span of the console, but nobody really cared. For many gamers in Korea, owning a pirated video game console and software titles became the status quo.

GAME ARCADES AND THE TIGER MOTHER

On the one hand, we had game consoles for home entertainment. On the other, we had game arcades that were also popular.

The small town in Seoul where I lived in had about four game arcades, most of them in a run-down state that conveyed a perfect sense of faded glamor to young gamers. The most popular titles were fighting games such as *Street Fighter 2*, *The King of Fighters*, *Tekken*, *Virtua Fighter*, and *Samurai Shodown*, along with some all-time classics like *Dungeons & Dragons* (an action-adventure game) and *Strikers 1945* (a shooting game). It was very cheap to play a round of most arcade games: normally one hundred KRW (South Korean won; equivalent to less than ten cents at today's KRW–USD exchange rate). In other words, teenage gamers

---

[1] For the record, I despised the lack of authenticity of the dark side. I couldn't accept the fact that I was playing a pirated version of the game. In my mind, it was disrespectful to the game creators, who had presumably spent years developing a virtual world, complete with characters and spectacularly absorbing storylines. I couldn't ride the dark side of the train.

could collect all the unnoticed coins around their home and use the proceeds to pay a visit to a local arcade.

The average age of gamers at the arcades was fairly low. Most people were teenagers, and there were very few adults. Every once in a while, however, the average age spiked when an angry mom entered the dark and soggy arcade room, suspicious that her beloved son might be skipping after-school classes.[2]

A friend of mine who went to after-school swimming classes every day, mainly thanks to the determination of his mother, skipped his routine one day. Instead, we went to a game arcade and ended up staying a little longer than we originally intended.

His mother was notorious as a tiger mom, long before that phrase became common parlance in the United States. She showed up suddenly in the arcade, her face betraying a hint of wrath. The moment she spotted her son innocently focused on his favorite shooting game, *Strikers 1945*, her rage instantly quadrupled.

Everyone in the arcade watched, aware that they were about to witness a familiar mother-hunting-son scene as it evolved into a bloodbath. They were not disappointed. In

---

[2] Unfortunately, girls in the arcade were rarer than unicorns, at least in the part of town where I lived.

a split second, the mother managed to steal her son's chair, put him on his feet, and deftly snatch the belt out of his trousers with the panache of a grandmaster martial artist at a public demonstration. The spectators in the arcade room were initially taken aback by the move, then realized that she was about to employ the belt as an implement of punishment.

The sound of the belt whipping against my friend's backside resonated around the room, capturing the attention of everyone in the arcade. After a few minutes of punishment, the tiger mother removed her son from the arcade, probably either to swimming class or back home to continue his punishment. The collective of video gamers took a moment of silence to digest what they had seen. Then they returned to their games.

PERSONAL COMPUTERS AND THE INTERNET

As a home video game market, South Korea was game-console-centric until the mid-nineties, with arcades for shared video gaming experiences. Since then, the market has shifted to PC gaming, to the extent that Korea later led the PC-game-centric esports scene. How did this happen? There were several factors.

MANDATORY COMPUTER EDUCATION AT KOREAN PUBLIC SCHOOLS

In 1987, the South Korean Ministry of Education initiated a mandatory curriculum on understanding computers for all pre-college students. As a result, public schools in Korea have gradually implemented computer courses into their curriculum since the early nineties. When I was a student, we learned about the overall structure of PCs, their components, and the role of each component, along with some elementary programming skills.

My first memory of computer education was in 1991, when I was in second grade. We were relocated to a newly built computer lab in the school, where each of us was allocated a PC during the class. First, we learned how to position our fingertips on the right places on the keyboard, so we could type quickly and accurately. This was the focus of our midterm exam; we were evaluated on how fast we could type, using a type-practicing program.

HOME PCS BECAME UBIQUITOUS

If pirated game consoles and game arcades were the common go-to options for game-loving kids in the mid-nineties, computer games were less common but growing in popularity. These PCs were initially bought primarily for work-related activities, not for entertainment purposes.

Then they became the new piece of "furniture" that everyone wanted to have in their home.

I was lucky enough to have one. My first PC was a 286 that my dad bought around the time I started attending computer education classes at school. I remember my only interest in the strange boxy-looking machine was playing games such as *Prince of Persia* (an epic) and *Tetris*. While I was not the only one among my friends who had a PC in the home, I was probably on the early adopter side. Parents in a PC-owning household may have used the computers primarily for non-entertainment reasons (documentation, programming, design, etc.), but the kids in the house quickly learned that these machines were a perfect platform for gaming.

GREATER GAME PRODUCTION AND PIRACY

As new PCs with better specs (e.g., 386, 486, Pentiums) were introduced into the market, so was new computer game software. The graphics became more realistic; the sounds grew more vivid; many new game genres came into existence. I still remember my initial sensation when I played a game called *Doom*, an early first-person shooter, for the first time. It scared the crap out of me. As the library of available games grew, more and more people had access to them, virtually for free, thanks to the ubiquity of software piracy in the Korean market.

MODEMS, LAN, AND ONLINE GAMES

Before the internet really took off, in the mid-nineties Korea had a service called PC Communication.[3] PC Communication was a portal service based on telecommunication networks that was accessed via the public switched telephone network (PSTN) or through good old dial-up modems. These PC Communication channels provided the basis for online games such as online RPGs, which many people could play at the same time. These soon became increasingly popular; I'll explore the movement in more detail in later chapters.

ECONOMIC CONDITIONS IN SOUTH KOREA PRIOR TO THE BIRTH OF ESPORTS

September 2, 1997 was a day that changed the economic landscape of South Korea. The International Monetary Fund (IMF) intervened in the Korean economy, with the result that millions of people were laid off.

Many unemployed fathers were looking desperately for jobs or business opportunities to stabilize the finances of their household. The lucky ones had a chunk of cash they had received as severance pay from former employers, which gave them a shot at setting up their own business.

Some invested their severance fund in starting a restaurant

---

3   PC통신 in Korean. Popular ones at the time were Chollian, HiTEL, and Nownuri.

business—fried chicken restaurants were especially popular.[4] Some started a cab business. But some fathers didn't want to play it safe. They had the entrepreneurial mindset and the guts to try something new, and they struck out into a completely new line of business. This engagement of entrepreneurial talent became one of the key factors in the forthcoming boom of the South Korean esports industry, a dynamic I'll discuss further in chapter 4.

In summary, the South Korea of the nineties had a young game-loving generation who grew up with Japanese game consoles but were gradually shifting, thanks to the PCs appearing in households around the country and the advent of the telecommunication-based early form internet, toward online PC gaming.

At the same time, a generation of working-class parents was struggling as the nation hit a historic economic crisis. One consequence of this crisis was a surfeit of laid-off fathers, some of whom had severance packages and lots of time at their disposal. This was the weather at the verge of the birth of what the present-day generation now refers to simply as esports.

The next question, then, is how did PC games comprehensively overtake consoles at the head of the gaming market?

---

4 Rumor has it that there are more fried chicken restaurants in South Korea than there are McDonald's in the world.

To answer that question, we need to understand more about the games themselves.

CHAPTER 3

THE ONLINE GAMING BOOM

There are many genres of games. Shitloads of them.

But you don't need to know all of them. At this point, you only need to know about two. These two genres matter disproportionately because they have made direct contributions to the creation of esports in South Korea. They are:

- Massively multiplayer online role-playing games (MMORPGs)
- Real-time strategy (RTS) games

If you already understand these games, you may wish to skip this chapter. Assuming that you are not familiar at all, I'm going to attempt the most challenging part of this book for me as a writer—explaining entire genres of games to a complete beginner without using the game itself for illustration purposes.

It's like trying to explain what basketball is to someone who has never seen a basketball game. No matter how good the written explanation, it will never be as clear as watching people play basketball; a half-baked description could create an erroneous impression that will stick in the reader's head forever. I'll do my best to do the subject justice. Please bear with me.

MMORPG

In the video gaming world, role-playing games are common. Each player controls a specific character within the game world, where there are many adventures to be had, storylines to uncover, and monsters to vanquish. In a game called *The Legend of Zelda*, for example, players control a character called Link.

In most RPGs, the player must achieve a goal, such as saving the world by slaughtering an evil villain. In *The Legend of Zelda*, you (as Link) must save Princess Zelda from a bad guy. As the game opens, however, Link is much too weak a character to tackle such a powerful enemy. He must battle countless monsters to grow stronger—to level up, in video game parlance.

As a player, your abilities within the game are defined

by various stats, such as your level of strength, health, and speed. Every time you kill a monster, you earn your character a certain number of experience points. As your experience increases, Link levels up, improving his stats and gaining the capacity to take on greater challenges.[1]

Sometimes killing a special monster affords players a special item, such as a weapon that significantly boosts attack status. The world is large and varied; some players enjoy completing the main quest as quickly as possible, while others like to collect all the special items in the game.

RPGs contain quests for players to follow, enabling them to level up appropriately; without these quests, the characters would remain too puny to defeat strong enemies. Eventually, a player who has completed many quests, usually by playing for hundreds of hours, will build a character strong enough to face the final bad guy, for example, a malicious dragon with a taste for beautiful human princesses.

Triumph in this final battle and you will be rewarded with an ending scene, such as a kiss from a happy and grateful princess. Wait, all those hours for just a virtual kiss? Yes, apparently so. Let me have a word with the developers.

Now you have some understanding of RPGs. MMORPGs

---

[1] It's like an airline mileage system. When you reach a certain level, you attain bronze, silver, and gold status, each one coming with additional perks.

are basically RPGs played online by many, many people simultaneously, each one controlling their own character. In MMORPGs, players team up to fight the bad guys (an activity known as "raiding"), and level up as a team. Each team member's character has different strengths and weaknesses, so teaming up is the best way to maximize the strengths and compensate for the weaknesses.

Thus, in-game online communication between team members is vital for strategy, planning, and coordination. This may take place via typing or talking. When I was playing in the nineties, the only form of in-game communication was through chat windows similar to instant messaging, but nowadays some games allow players to communicate by voice.

MMORPG LOVERS IN THE NINETIES

Back in the mid-nineties, when South Korea's online PC game scene—based on modems—was booming, MMORPGs took off in a big way. The features of these games were notoriously addictive, resulting in constantly busy household phone lines and astronomical monthly phone bills, not to mention a constant supply of irate mothers.

My favorite MMORPG was a Korean game called *Legend of Darkness*, by Nexon. One interesting feature of the game, which in my opinion ratcheted up the addictiveness factor, was the ability for male and female characters to form cyber-marriages.

I had a character named Syd Warrior, a male tank character,[2] and I happened to meet someone playing a female magician character named Bombshell.[3] We regularly raided together and got to know each other better through in-game chats. While I was a junior high schooler, the person playing as Bombshell told me she was four years older than me, officially an adult.

Around this time, my game-playing hours increased significantly, so much so that my mother often yelled at me. Coincidence? I think not. For the first time in my not-so-long gaming life—I was fifteen—I was in love.

The tedious raids required to level up suddenly felt like exciting online dates. I had never met Bombshell in person and online dating wasn't yet a common phenomenon, but we talked about numerous subjects, just like a normal couple, all while growing our characters together in the game world.

From our online connection, Bombshell and I naturally

---

[2] In the gaming world, players can choose the gender of their character. A surprising number of male players choose female avatars.

[3] 탱탱빵빵 in Korean, for the record.

progressed to talking on the phone at night. This was a sensational experience for me. Not only was I relieved to discover that the person behind the avatar was a real female human being, but I also learned that she had a beautiful voice over the phone. Raiding in *Legend of Darkness* and talking on the phone late at night, after my parents had gone to bed, robbed me of almost all my sleeping hours.

Eventually, Bombshell and I decided to meet offline. She kindly came all the way to the town where I lived. I, an innocent junior high schooler, was about to meet up with a self-employed female adult who worked at a clothing store.

The meeting was a shock. Bombshell was fully made up, which emphasized her adulthood. She also smoked quite heavily. After all the anticipation, meeting in person was extremely awkward. Neither of us knew what to do, so we went straight to a nearby underground *norae-bang* (karaoke room), a common form of entertainment in Korea. I sang for hours while Bombshell sat there, smoking.

Eventually, the awkward singing session concluded and we parted peacefully, assuring one another it was great to meet in person and promising to resume raiding as soon as we returned to our computers.

We never saw each other again, either in the real world or virtually.

REAL-TIME STRATEGY

Let's move on to real-time strategy (RTS) games. If there is one type of game that I need to explain to convey the realities of early esports in South Korea, it's RTS. This explanation may seem complex, but I'll do my best to make it as clear as possible.

Unlike MMORPGs, in which players fight *together* with other human players against programmed monsters, the entire premise of RTS is that players are on a battlefield with other gamers, fighting *against* them. Each player chooses a fictitious tribe or species to command, and the goal of the game is to defeat the other gamers' tribe on the battlefield, by outsmarting them. Players can play head-to-head, like chess, or play in teams, like basketball.

Let me elaborate on what it means to command a tribe. Players have control over every decision their tribe makes. Most RTS games rely on three modes of operations: resource collection, unit production, and combat. A player who collects more resources will be able to produce more units, giving them an advantage in combat.

Players begin with limited resources, so how they choose to allocate those resources determines how the game proceeds. With two human players matching up against each other, this can become a game of cat-and-mouse. One player may begin by collecting resources that will allow them to create better, stronger units. If the other player reads that strategy, however, their opponent may launch into combat and destroy the resource collection operation, possibly winning the match. Much like chess, the game ends when one player eliminates all of the other player's bases, or when one of the competitors surrenders.

WHY WAS *STARCRAFT* SO SPECIAL?

Hopefully, the primer above has given you a taste of what RTS games involve. Back in mid-nineties South Korea, people played several RTS games; most, such as *Age of Empires*, *Command & Conquer*, and *Warcraft II* were produced by US game publishers. South Koreans enjoyed these RTS games a great deal, partly because so many of us were familiar with strategy games thanks to epic quests like the *Romance of the Three Kingdoms* series by KOEI, a Japanese gaming company.[4]

In 1998, an American game company called Blizzard Entertainment—now Activision Blizzard—released a game called *StarCraft*. Wikipedia describes *StarCraft* as a science-fiction RTS game. Players can play as any one of three space tribes: Terran (human beings), Zerg (bugs), and Protoss

---

[4] Unlike RTS games from the United States, these Japanese games didn't feature a real-time element.

(aliens with high-tech civilization).[5] In Korea, the game was extremely well received.

I first played *StarCraft* through a classmate. My first impression was that it kept me busy all the time. And I mean *all* the time. There was so much to do. First, I used the basic labor units to collect resources, and then I decided which production line to build to grow the capacity to produce battle units. The game features at least a dozen different types of battle units, each one with unique capabilities and requiring specific resources to create. A key element of *StarCraft* is choosing the right combination of battle units to defeat one's opponent in combat.

Unlike RPGs or MMORPGs, in which the player controls only a single character, players in *StarCraft* control more than a hundred units simultaneously as the game progresses. To succeed, players need the ability to allocate attention and manage resources effectively, among other critical skillsets.

Why did Koreans enjoy playing *StarCraft* so much more than other RTS games? I don't have a definitive answer, but I can make some educated guesses. In comparison with other RTS games, *StarCraft* was relatively fast-paced. When I first played *Command & Conquer*, there were fun

---

[5] In case you are familiar with cheap Hollywood flicks, it's similar to *Starship Troopers* (human versus bugs) with a side order of *Predator* (high-tech aliens).

game factors, but the overall pace of the game was rather slow. South Koreans are famous for our love of speed or, less kindly, our impatience. I think this *pali-pali*[6] element of Korean mentality matched the pace of *StarCraft*'s gameplay.

Second, the quality of a battle game is defined by the balance between the species. If one type of Terran battle unit had even a small advantage over a Protoss unit of matching rank, the gameplay would have quickly become lopsided. Thanks to the hard work of the game designers and developers, *StarCraft*'s three space species were perfectly balanced.

Third, the reaction time of the player-controlled units was quite fast, enabling players to perform a micro-control,[7] increasing the fun and generating a small combat advantage. I still remember when I first saw a micro-control technique, now common in *StarCraft*,[8] performed for the first time by a player sitting next to me. I was shocked. The micro-controls were subtle enough to allow for constant improvement. Soon after I first saw someone using micro-control, I was trying the same move on my own.

Fourth, *StarCraft* provided online servers, called battle.

---

6 Literally means "hurry-hurry" in Korean.

7 A micro-control is a fine maneuver made by a skilled player. Using a mouse on one hand and a keyboard command on the other, the player controls his game units with expert precision and timing. For a player to reach this level requires a lot of effort.

8 The move was called a "Reever drop." I won't explain it in detail.

net, where anybody in the world with a network connection could log in and play against other people. The site featured leaderboards, taking the competition to the next level. No matter how good a player was, there was always a possibility they would come up against someone who could beat them.

Lastly, *StarCraft* had lots of room for strategy and tactics. When players selected a production line—issuing what was known as a build order—they determined the types of units they would be able to produce later in the game. As professional players took the game to the next level, it became obvious that players who chose their build orders wisely could reap a significant advantage in terms of units produced and timing.

A SIDE NOTE: POPULAR GAME GENRES IN PRESENT-DAY ESPORTS

MMORPGs and RTS games were outstandingly successful in the early days of the Korean esports scene. As the ecosystem evolved, however, two other genres of games became increasingly popular. If you are interested in present-day esports, it's worth understanding this progression. These genres are:

- First-person shooter (FPS)
- Multiplayer online battle arena (MOBA)

FIRST-PERSON SHOOTERS

If you have a teenage gamer kid in your household in 2020, there is a good chance that they are avidly playing at least one of these titles: *Fortnite Battle Royale, PlayerUnknown's Battlegrounds (PUBG), Overwatch, Valorant, Call of Duty (CoD), Counter-Strike: Global Offensive (CS:GO)*, or *Knives Out (荒野行動)*. These are all either FPS games or battle royale games, a variation of FPS.

Even if you haven't played any of these games, the concept of FPS is easy to understand. As a gamer, you control an avatar, for example, a militant in a war zone. Your aim is to destroy your opponent's avatar, much as you would do if you were fighting an enemy on an actual battlefield. You can utilize weapons such as machine guns, grenades, knives, and sometimes even missiles.

Traditional FPS games only allowed one player to play at a time. As the online PC game era progressed, however, FPSs evolved to embrace multiplayer capabilities. The most popular are online multiplayer battle royale games, such as *Fortnite* or *PUBG*, which allow as many as one hundred people to play against one another at the same time.

Most mainstream FPS games used to be played on PCs, but now they are gradually shifting to mobile devices such as smartphones. This makes them easy to download and play during a commute. In South Korea, you can easily find people playing FPSs on public transportation in cities or see groups of friends gathered in local fast-food chains to access the free Wi-Fi and play games.

MULTIPLAYER ONLINE BATTLE ARENA

MOBA games include titles like *League of Legends* and *Dota 2*. Think of MOBA as a lovechild of RTS and MMORPG. MOBA is considered a type of RTS, like *StarCraft*, because it is a real-time strategy game. But, as the acronym suggests, MOBA games support multiple players—usually teams of five versus five—by default, unlike the *StarCraft*-like RTS games, where most people play one versus one in a professional scene.

As one member of a five-member team, players choose a character (or "champion") from more than a hundred options. Just like in MMORPGs, each champion has unique characteristics and capabilities, represented by their stats.

By teaming up with other champions, players become part of a team. In combination, the five champions should complement each other's strengths and balance each other's weaknesses.[9] Just like in MMORPGs, each champion can level up, either by killing opposing champions or by hunting

---

9   Let me give you a crude analogy using the *Lord of the Rings* movie series. If Frodo, a hobbit, teams up with Aragorn, a human, and Gimli, a dwarf, Team Frodo may be strong in close combat but dreadful at long range. If Frodo swaps Gimli for the pretty-boy elf Legolas, who is capable of long-range arrow attacks, Team Frodo is more balanced in both close combat and long-range attacks.

down antagonistic "minions," who are similar to pawns in chess. At higher levels, champions gain more skills. Champions can also earn gold, which serves as currency, by defeating opponents. Gold allows champions to purchase items that boost their stats.[10]

The goal of the game genre is to demolish the opposing team's main structure, which is located at the heart of their base. At the beginning of the game, each team starts close to their own base, on a map showing three routes—top, mid, and bottom. Each champion is situated on one route, meaning that players may face a number of opposing champions along the route they are guarding. This structure brings up various questions and invites different strategies. For example, who goes to which route, and when? Who helps whom in case of emergency?

What makes this game crazily addictive is the infinite number of possible strategic and tactical combinations, depending on the players' choice of champion, their team members' choices, and the combination employed by the opponents' team. The impact of various items adds another layer of complexity and fun.

---

10   If Aragorn collects a lot of gold by killing many orcs, he is able to buy Anduril, the sword that killed Sauron.

PC BANGS COMPLETE THE SHIFT TO PC GAMING

MMORPG was the genre that introduced many gamers to the online PC space. Arguably, Korean gamers gained their online literacy through MMORPGs.

But MMORPGs were never suited to esports because the games weren't designed for one-on-one competition.[11] On the other hand, RTS games like *StarCraft* always featured battles between players. It was easy to adapt them to an esports world. In an era when artificial intelligence was less advanced than it is today, defeating human players was an order of magnitude more challenging than beating the computer. That additional challenge meant more fun.

As kids in South Korea became enthusiastic about games that were available exclusively for PCs, the game industry in the country shifted from Japanese game consoles to American PC games.

Was that enough to popularize esports? In hindsight, probably not. In the late nineties, gamers were still only a small fraction of the Korean population. *StarCraft* was popular among gamers but irrelevant to those who didn't own PCs.

Remember the laid-off fathers and their severance pack-

---

11 Yes, one may argue that players could "compete" with other peers by comparing how many levels they had gained, the monsters they had killed, and the fancy items they collected, but MMORPGs were not designed for peer-to-peer (p2p) competition.

ages? They were about to change the South Korean gaming landscape by creating a new business model. When this business model caught on, PC gaming was no longer a luxury for the few. It was a big part of the life of the average Korean teenager.

The new businesses opened by the entrepreneurial fathers of South Korea were known as PC bangs. They would revolutionize the gaming industry in the country and pave the way for the success of esports.

CHAPTER 4

KARAOKE? NO, PC BANGS

One drawback of playing online PC games at home was that, because gameplay was based on telecommunication-based modems, it occupied household phone lines, usually for hours. This caused phone bills to skyrocket and enraged mothers. For gamers, getting scolded was an occupational hazard.

Fortunately, the situation moved in a favorable direction for gaming when high-speed cable internet became available. Some business-savvy people noticed that online PC gaming was rapidly gaining popularity among the young generation in South Korea, even though relatively few people had a networked PC at home. There was clearly a gap in the market, catering to people who wanted to play online PC games but did not have PCs at home.

Some of the people who were laid off due to the Korean financial crisis spotted this gap and espied a new type of business opportunity, different from the standard path of fried chicken parlor owners and cab drivers. Many of these people felt that they had nothing to lose. The economic environment was so bad that some even committed suicide; many of those who chose to live were willing to take a risk in the hope of turning their lives around.

These were the circumstances that led to the birth of PC bangs.[1] Some people took their severance pay and opened up facilities at shopping arcades. They purchased or rented several high-spec PCs and subscribed to super-fast internet networks. The concept was similar to the internet cafe, but this new business model was different. Customers didn't visit PC bangs for a quick internet search (AltaVista, anybody?) or to perform some business administration. Instead, they went to play games.

PC BANGS: COMMODITIZED GAME SERVICE AND COMMUNITY BUILDING

As described in previous chapters, several factors influenced the extent to which South Korea became a PC-centric gaming market. The availability of PCs, local area networks

---

[1] Koreans love to go to karaoke, but we call it *norae-bang*. *Norae* means "songs" and *bang* means "room." A song room. We soon named the new gaming cafes PC bangs, meaning "a room with PCs."

(LANs), affordable high-speed internet, and the availability of pirated offline and online game software all played a part.

But what really changed the scene was the advent of PC bangs. When game-dedicated net cafes began to spring up around the country, gamers no longer needed the best PC and network environment at home. Nor did they need to get hold of the latest game software through some shady piracy site. As long as they paid a few bucks per hour,[2] they could play any game they wanted, whenever they desired.

Another bonus of the new ecosystem was that it naturally enabled the formation of local communities. For young gamers, it was always fun to play with friends. Even those who didn't know anyone could make new friends at PC bangs. Some gamers continued to play at home on their own PCs, but most of us played at PC bangs. The PC bang business started slightly before the time *StarCraft* was released in 1998, so the timing was perfect.

Schoolkids went crazy playing *StarCraft* at PC bangs. In the afternoons, PC bangs were packed with kids who had come straight from school, complete with backpacks and lunch bags. Were there also adults? Absolutely. The service was cost-effective, there was entertainment at hand, the facilities were cozy, and there was food available, a combination that made PC bangs appealing to adults as well as kids.

---

2   The standard rate was about two USD per hour.

In addition to being a place to play games, PC bangs were also a place to spectate. If a good player showed up, people would gather around to watch, screaming in awe at his control technique or game strategy. Throughout the nation, PC bangs were a major success. It seemed as though literally everyone was playing *StarCraft* in PC bangs. I went to a male-only junior high and high school in Seoul, and it was extremely hard to find *anybody* who did not play *StarCraft*.[3]

JUMPING OUT OF WINDOWS

When teenagers get obsessed by a new craze, emotions run high. I was no exception. One day, my buddy (let me call him Juan) and I, both high schoolers, decided to hang out at my place and play games. I had a decent PC with a network in my room, so Juan often came over to my place and we took turns until pretty late at night.

My neighborhood was a place called Banpo, an area in the heart of Seoul now better known as "Gangnam," due to a funny Korean artist who happens to have attended the same high school as Juan and I did.[4] Overall, it was a small, peaceful town (walking from one end of the town to the

---

[3] Perhaps because we were male only, we had nothing else more exciting to do. It's possible that games were less popular in mixed-sex schools.

[4] Side note: he showed up as an alumnus at our school festival one day, wearing his school uniform, and performed an incredibly dirty dance in front of the entire school of male-only students and teachers. This was waaaaay before he achieved global stardom with his mega hit song, "Gangnam Style."

other only took fifteen to twenty minutes, tops)—seemingly too peaceful to be located in the heart of Seoul.

Then the town was hit by a sudden PC-bang boom. Even in a small town like Banpo, we had six PC bangs on one block, operating night and day, sucking in the pocket money of the neighborhood's kids like a vacuum cleaner. Juan and I happened to be two of those kids.

No parent really appreciated the idea of their kids spending hours at a PC bang, but that didn't prevent us from flouting the rules whenever possible. I only had one PC and Juan and I got tired of waiting for a turn, so we came up with a brilliant idea: sneaking out of the apartment after my parents fell asleep, spending all night at a PC bang,[5] and returning silently before they woke up in the morning.

My parents' bedroom lay between my bedroom and the exit, so we came up with what we thought was a brilliant plan. Why bother passing through their bedroom, and risk unlocking and locking the entrance door lock? We might wake my parents. Our apartment was on the second floor, so we decided to simply jump out of the window of my room.

We waited until my parents were asleep, brought our shoes to my room, and jumped out of the window, one by one. Despite our expectation that jumping from the second floor

---

[5] PC bangs even offered a "late-night special" promotion to attract folks like us.

would be safe, looking down at the ground from a second-floor window was quite scary. I dangled out of the window, stretching my arms as much as I could to maximize my body length and minimize the distance I was going to free-fall.

I remember that, as I let go, the free-falling time was much longer than I had anticipated. I even had time to think, "Why am I still falling?" Then I touched down, hitting the ground with my butt. Surprisingly, that didn't really hurt. Juan closed the window behind him, then leaped after me in a similar fashion. The next thing we knew, both of us were out in the street in the middle of the night.

We felt a sense of freedom we had never known before—think Tim Robbins in *The Shawshank Redemption*—and rushed straight to our destination, where we played games all night as we'd envisioned.[6] That was how important PC bangs were to teenagers.[7]

---

[6] Epilogue #1: We were so excited about our plan that we completely forgot to figure out how we'd get back into the house. We overlooked the fact that we needed to get *back* to my room, which entailed unlocking the door, traversing my parents' room, and inevitably waking them up. When we came back the next morning, we were caught. Juan swiftly went home. After he left, my mom beat the crap out of me and grounded me for a few days.

[7] Epilogue #2: The following day, both Juan and I suffered from an excruciating ache in the muscles of our bellies and butts. We believe it was the aftermath of the free fall. Nonetheless, I'm glad we did what we did. Even more than two decades later, I remember it vividly, and here I am telling the story to promote esports.

FOOD AT PC BANGS

As growing teenagers, we needed to eat all the time. We spent many hours in PC bangs, so we got hungry. The owners of PC bangs were happy to cater to our culinary needs.

Initially, the food menus consisted of simple, cheap, ready-made Korean snacks, such as dried squid and dried corn, along with soda-pop vending machines. Later, the bangs stocked instant cup ramen noodles and prepared hot water. We Koreans love our cup noodles, so this was a smart move. The cup noodles only cost us maybe a buck or two, so even as hungry teenagers, we could easily pay out of our pocket money.

From the perspective of PC bang proprietors, noodles have another advantage. They smell delicious. When someone had a portion of ramen noodles in the sealed space of a PC bang, the appetizing smell quickly filled the room. Gradually, one gamer after another took a break and grabbed a packet of noodles. Pretty soon, the entire bang was full of teenagers slurping ramen noodles.

It's funny how habits endure. There are only a few PC bangs in Tokyo, so few that I could count the number on my fingers. Recently, my colleagues and I visited one. As soon as we sat down, we were irresistibly drawn to order a cup of ramen noodles.[8]

Long before the launch of Uber Eats, South Korea was already a hotbed of food delivery. This made ordering in another option for hungry patrons of PC bangs. The most popular choices were Korean/Chinese-style noodles, called *jajangmyeon*, and Korean fried chicken.[9]

The combination of gaming and good food—especially *jajangmyeon*[10]—was highly fulfilling. Imagine playing your favorite game with buddies while eating one of your favorite dishes. It was a sensation of pure happiness. Time flew.

PC BANGS: A BUSINESS PERSPECTIVE

Owning a PC bang was an easy way for people to set up in business, so the numbers grew rapidly.[11] Within Banpo, the town where I lived, there were five schools for primary education (one elementary, two junior highs, and two high

---

[8] And, thank god, they offered the right selection of ramen! Cup ramen noodles at PC bangs are like any other great combination: burgers with French fries and Coke, yakitori with cold draft beer (or *nama-biru*), *samgyupsal* with Korean *soju*.

[9] Delivery guys will deliver anywhere in Korea. There used to be a TV commercial parodying the Korean delivery-guy mentality that was extremely popular for a while. Ironically, the commercial itself was for a telecom service. Delivering to a PC bang must have been a piece of cake for the delivery guys.

[10] You'll know what I mean if you are Korean or have fallen in love with this thing before.

[11] According to a report by the Korea Creative Content Agency (KOCCA), the number peaked in 2001 with 23,548 PC bangs. That is about the same number of 7-Elevens in Japan.

schools). Two of the five were only for females. There were six PC bang facilities.[12] Most of the time, the bangs were packed with male schoolkids. In those early days, an interesting aspect of the PC bang business was that few establishments pursued aggressive marketing campaigns. Recommendations came mostly via word of mouth.

The PC bangs in Banpo ranged in size from twenty PCs to almost a hundred. The clerk at the counter assigned them manually, on a first-come-first-serve basis. When gameplay started, the clerk noted down the time. When customers left, they gave their seat number to the cashier and paid for the time they had used.

It was a simple business model, running 24/7 with no holiday closures.[13] Some PC bangs offered special night-owl packages from 12 a.m. to 6 a.m. for a fixed price of ten dollars, like the one Juan and I took advantage of when we sneaked out to play all night.

In present-day Korea, the PC bang business is still going strong. More than two decades since its birth, the business has evolved considerably. When more female customers started to show up at PC bangs in the mid-2000s, as the

---

[12] After a heated discussion with old friends, including Juan, we have concluded that there were at least six: in alphabetical order, BattleZone, Click, Episode, Highway, Link, and Mega Web Station.

[13] In fact, the holiday season was busier because young relatives all got together and went to PC bangs.

best esports players rose to stardom—a phenomenon I'll discuss further in chapter 6—the overall interior design and the sanitary level of the facilities went up a notch to meet their needs.

LOCAL TOURNAMENTS AT PC BANGS

The best game players in the area became locally famous. Novices and mediocre players gathered around the local celebrities, either to learn from their strategies or simply because watching them play was entertaining. The vibe was similar to the game arcades where young spectators gathered around a good match of *Street Fighter*, *Tekken*, or *Mortal Kombat*.

In every class at my school, there was someone who was pretty good at *StarCraft*. That player soon found themselves surrounded by a new circle of friends who wanted to watch them play and compete against them. Some students devoted too much time to games, intentionally skipping more serious after-school activities, such as attending cram schools. Academic achievement is prized highly in Korea, and there were cram schools dedicated to every imaginable subject (math, Korean, English, science, etc.). Occasionally, angry mothers in search of their missing sons poked their heads into PC bangs, but I never witnessed another belt-whipping episode.

As PC bang owners witnessed the boom they were a part

of, some started to organize tournaments. In part, this was because the market was quickly in danger of becoming saturated. New PC bangs were opening up regularly, and the owners needed differentiating factors to stand out from their competitors. The hardware and software were the same (in the early days of PC gaming there weren't many models with higher or lower specs), as were the food and beverages. Savvy owners needed a new way to promote their PC bang above others.

Naturally, the prizes were much more moderate than the multimillion-dollar awards available to winners of today's international tournaments, but victors received cash prizes (of around $1,000) or a good chunk of coupons for free use of the organizer's PC bang. That was enough to attract local contenders.

Hosting tournaments was a smart move on the part of PC bang owners. First, by throwing local events, they created a buzz around their PC bang, amounting to a form of free marketing. Second, tournaments were quite cheap for owners. Giving out free coupons cost them no more than the price of the electricity to run the PCs. Thanks to the free hours, tournament winners usually became dedicated customers of the bang where they had triumphed, probably bringing their circle of friends along for the ride.

Before long, PC bang proprietors throughout the nation

began to hold tournaments, some relatively big, others relatively small.

STARCRAFT ON TV

Local tournaments gave my friends and me an appetite for competitive gaming. But we never imagined they would grow to the status of national championships. That is, until we saw people on television playing *StarCraft* professionally.

Can you imagine the sensations we felt? Out of the blue, our favorite game was on television. Gamers were competing with each other just like professional sportspeople, complete with casters and commentators.

What the heck was happening?

CHAPTER 5

ESPORTS ON CABLE

Late one afternoon, I returned from school, unloaded my backpack, and turned on the television in the living room. Thanks to my parents, we had recently subscribed to a cable TV network with dozens of channels.[1] As a cable TV newbie, I navigated my way through what felt like a nearly infinite number of channels. Movie channel; next. Sports channel; next. Professional go channel; popular among fathers, but a definite next for me.

Suddenly, I stopped clicking and stared open-mouthed at the television. I could not believe what I was seeing. A one-on-one game of *StarCraft* was on TV.

Initially, I thought I'd stumbled across some sort of

---

1 Korea used to broadcast five channels (SBS, KBS1, KBS2, MBC, and EBS), but only three of them showed anything entertaining.

localized commercial made by Blizzard, the publisher of *StarCraft*. Soon, however, it became obvious that wasn't the case. The camera angle shifted from the game screen to the players. They were oddly dressed, like budget characters in *Mad Max*. Each one wore a headset and sat in front of a decorated PC. They appeared to be engaged in a serious *StarCraft* duel.

This was interesting enough, but when I listened carefully, I could hear commentators explaining what was happening in the game. One explained the facts and game decisions of the players, while another interpreted what those decisions might mean to the outcome of the game. After the match, the camera angle switched to the caster and the commentators, who briefed viewers on the result of the game and the overall story. The broadcast gave the unmistakable impression of a professional sports match.

ONGAMENET: WHY WAS IT FUN TO WATCH?

When I collected myself and understood what I was seeing, it became apparent that I had stumbled onto the very first dedicated esports channel on Korean cable television. It was called OnGameNet.[2]

To a schoolkid like myself, the whole experience was shock-

---

[2] In 2015, they changed their name to OGN.

ing, but some aspects were more shocking than others. In particular:

- *StarCraft* was on TV.
- The entire channel was dedicated to esports and related subjects.
- The guys playing *StarCraft* were dressed in weird costumes.
- There were casters and commentators explaining what was happening to spectators.
- The commentary made the viewing experience more entertaining.
- The players were really, really good; better than anyone at my local PC bang.

HOW DID ONGAMENET START?

In 1998, the year the World Cup was held in France and won by the hosts, a junior TV producer on a channel called Tooniverse had an idea. The idea was to broadcast a show predicting the results of the World Cup, using a popular soccer simulation video game. The entire nation was gripped by World Cup fever, so this seemed like a great idea, although the South Korean national team had failed to qualify for the last sixteen.

The show was the first time video games were presented like sports on Korean television. For a better viewing experience, the channel hired a cyber caster and human commentators to talk people through the action in the soccer simulation game. The game ended up correctly predicting the match outcomes more frequently than the producer had anticipated.

Excited by the result, the TV station extended the prediction format to baseball. Back then, Park Chan Ho, a legendary South Korean baseball pitcher, played in the MLB. Many people followed his career, so it was natural to apply the same format to predict the results of his games.

Then the show's producer, Mr. Hwang Hyung Jun, noticed the nationwide *StarCraft*/PC-bang boom. He immediately saw the potential, so he pivoted the game-prediction channel format toward *StarCraft* broadcasting. And lo and behold. The birth of OnGameNet.

FROM LOCAL TO NATIONAL

The small esports tournaments held routinely at local PC bangs were fun events, great for business owners and enjoyable for PC bang users. But these tournaments were limited to local participants.

An esports-only TV channel, on the other hand, required content that could attract viewers nationwide. Korea had already embraced esports tournaments locally and—thanks to the local tournaments—many people were already familiar with the format. That made them perfect to meet OnGameNet's needs. The channel gathered together the best *StarCraft* players in the nation, pitted them against each other in a tournament, and broadcasted the results.

Although the first tournament I watched on OnGameNet only featured a few participants, it was fascinating to see how each player had a unique playing style and strategy. The commentators gave each player a nickname, which made the watching experience even more fun. For instance, there was a Zerg user who was nicknamed the "Sauron Zerg," because his playing style resembled that of another famous online player with the ID Sauron.[3]

ESPORTS CHAMPION ON TV COMMERCIALS

OnGameNet was a cable channel. It was only available to cable subscribers. But one professional esports player made it to Korean national television as the main character in a major communication company's commercial.[4] At the time, most TV commercials used big-shot celebrities to sell their

---

[3] In other words, he was good at rapidly expanding his hatchery bases. Another Zerg guy, whose name I won't mention to protect his honor, sported facial features that strangely resembled the Zerg's.

[4] Lee Gi Seok, also known by his ID SSamjang, won Blizzard's 1999 *StarCraft* ladder tournament, making him an official world champion. The commercial was for Korea Telecom and was broadcast in 1999.

products, so it was shocking to see an esports player placed in the same bracket.[5]

For game lovers in Korea, this was a magical period. Negative perceptions of gaming and gamers were slowly changing, and this commercial was evidence of the transition. Traditionally, gamers were expected to reside far from the highly motivated, extroverted over-achievers in the darkest part of society, in the far corner of some dank PC bang or the shadiest room of their parents' apartment. Suddenly, we found ourselves in the spotlight of a somewhat conservative South Korean society.

CREATING AN ATMOSPHERE

If you watched a professional sports match on TV, you would find it odd if there were no casters and commentators interpreting the game. These folks provide a great deal of background information regarding the match, the team, the athletes, the history, etc. The game would be less entertaining without them. The caster and the pundit complement each other, with former pro athletes offering insights into, for example, the mentality of players as they make certain decisions and movements.

The same applies to the esports scene. The very first

---

[5] I'm pretty sure many people watching the commercial for the first time thought, "Who's this guy and why is he starring in this commercial?"

StarCraft League, broadcast in 1999, utilized the same caster-commentator set up as a normal sports program. Indeed, esports casters and commentators were doing a brand-new job, presenting professional esports. How cool is that?

Nowadays, online streaming services use a similar setup. I attended the *Tekken* World Final event in Amsterdam in 2018, which was sponsored and broadcasted by Twitch. For that tournament, there were actually four people on the commentary team, a caster and three commentators, each one describing the key moments in one-on-one *Tekken* matches lasting a few minutes each.

The beauty of the caster-commentator setup is the buildup of emotion as the game progresses. It's normal for commentators to suddenly burst out shouting as if they cannot believe what they are seeing. In *StarCraft*, that could be caused by a hidden bunker rush by a Terran player, a hidden hatchery built by a Zerg player in a blind spot right behind an opponent's base, or a Protoss player unveiling a group of carriers that even the commentator didn't notice.[6] This list can go on and on.

Another excuse for an eruption is a player's use of the acronym GG, meaning "good game." When esports became

---

6   Speaking of commentators going nuts over a hidden carrier, here is a good example from YouTube: https://youtu.be/dK99iOh5Ico

popular on TV, players who were about to lose a game took to writing "GG" in the game chat as an acknowledgment of defeat.

This made for dramatic moments. A sudden announcement of GG, especially after a fierce match between professional players, broke the tension and encouraged the casters, commentators, and members of the audience to scream like ecstatic soccer fans who had just witnessed a goal for their team in a UEFA Champions League final.

THE STAR CASTERS

As well as star players, the new esports ecosystem had space for star casters and commentators. These folks paved the way for esports to become a solid spectator sport. There are several casters and commentators who I hold in high regard. Let me begin with the casters.

Jung Il Hoon was probably the first esports caster in Korea. He looked more like a news anchorman than a typical esports caster because he seemed scholarly, wore glasses, and always had a hint of a smile, like a fatherly figure from the church. When he first appeared on TV as an esports caster, he seemed out of place. My friends and I wondered why someone as old as our dads was commenting on a game that, we assumed, he barely understood. Although his grown-up look did not seem to match gaming culture, he provided a sense of stability. His presence, his tone, and the delivery of his comments gave viewers the feeling that it was okay to watch competitive gaming for hours. Following the conclusion of his career as a caster, he now works with a major media content production company.[7]

Jeon Yong Jun has had perhaps the longest career in the Korean esports scene, easily more than a decade. He was one of the main casters during the era of the *StarCraft* League. Now that *StarCraft* League is no more, he has continued as the main anchorman of *League of Legends* broadcasts. In comparison with Mr. Jung, he is more emotional. His laid-back character, liking for cracking jokes, and signature agitated yell at climactic moments make him entertaining to watch and relatable to fans of games. In many ways, he seems like a big brother.

There have been a few female casters too, although not many. The most notable is Jung Sorim. Besides her age-defying beauty, she is an irreplaceable figure in esports broadcasting who has paved the way for subsequent female casters. Being a mother of a game-loving son, she has also appeared on different variety shows where she has shared her tips on how to parent gamers wisely for a peaceful household—and no more angry grandmothers. Her affection for games and players was confirmed when she burst into tears when a Korean team recorded victory at

---

[7] Namuwiki page: 정일훈(방송인)

a major international esports tournament for the first time in seven years.[8] She has recently started a Twitch channel of her own.

THE STAR COMMENTATORS

There have also been star esports commentators, beginning with the duo of Um Ki Young and Kim "Carry" Tae Hyung. Mr. Um is the oldest commentator on the Korean esports scene and found his vocation completely by chance. Mr. Um and the producer who created OnGameNet were both alumni of the same university. When Mr. Um visited the broadcasting channel for unrelated reasons—prior to becoming a commentator he used to be a cartoonist—the two chatted about the producer's new game channel. The producer knew that Mr. Um was good at commenting and interpreting, so he offered Mr. Um a job. And indeed, Mr. Um was good.[9]

When a match began, Mr. Um spoke calmly, as though he were reciting a lullaby. Like other commentators, however, he often became agitated as the match progressed. By utilizing the storytelling talents he had developed as a cartoonist, he was very good at crafting a narrative during the match. He gave many star players nicknames, which have stayed with them to this day. His commentary turned

---

8   The actual footage is here: https://www.youtube.com/watch?v=H9BQIlho_-c&feature=youtu.be

9   Namuwiki page: 엄재경

what would have otherwise been ordinary games between two game fanatics into thrilling stories of duels between fully realized characters, each with background stories to share and reasons behind their determination to win. Mr. Um played an essential part in placing Korean esports on an equal footing with watching spectacular sports matches. I believe he is no longer active, but many of us still remember his commentary.

In the early days of esports, Mr. Um was joined for almost every match by another legendary commentator. Before joining the esports scene, Mr. Kim was a licensed golf instructor. Due to the IMF financial crisis that shook the South Korean economy in 1997, he needed to find a new job. He ended up working at a PC bang, where he grew to love *StarCraft*. Soon, he became an avid player, winning many online battles and ultimately a championship. As a result of this triumph, Mr. Kim was invited to become a *StarCraft* commentator.[10]

Mr. Kim's overall commentary style of speech was also relatively calm and quiet. He commented only when necessary, occasionally offering harsh but fair feedback about the play of the competitors. He was usually the straight guy in the three-person commentary setup, maintaining a poker face

---

10 Namuwiki page: 김태형(1973)

while Mr. Um and the caster were happy to laugh their asses off about events on the screen.[11]

Mr. Um and Mr. Kim were the first two legends, but there were many more. Lee Seung Won was probably the most accurate commentator of all time. Then there were former pro athletes turned commentators, such as Kim Jung Min, Lim Sung Chun, and Kim Dong Jun.

THE DREAM OF GOING PROFESSIONAL

The new esports ecosystem seemed to have everything: a game that captured the imagination, PC bangs where people spent hours crafting their *StarCraft* skills,[12] and now a dedicated esports cable channel with a nationwide audience. The esports industry was born, and with more and more players and viewers pulled in as time went by, it seemed that the industry would go from strength to strength.

What was still missing? The prospect of professionalism. Although the tournament events attracted good players, the winners weren't accorded enough social recognition

---

[11] There was one event, however, that excited even Mr. Poker Face: when a Protoss player decided to produce the most expensive battle unit: the carrier, an airborne battleship that deploys a swarm of smaller ships. Carriers are a costly unit whose manufacture involves quite a risk to the player, so this did not happen very often. But when it did, Mr. Kim could not resist yelling, "The carrier has arrived!!" This is how he got the nickname Kim Carry.

[12] Side note: even in front of Korean military bases, there were many PC bangs.

to make gaming a serious career option. Serious players worked their butts off to win tournaments and claim moderate prize money, but that was as far as the ecosystem had progressed. Nobody in Korean society considered "gamer" a serious occupation.

Why would they? It was only a few years after *StarCraft*/PC bangs/OnGameNet had emerged. In most people's minds, gaming was still a guilty pleasure. Many people played games, and some even nurtured a secret passion for them, but that was all. Sadly, for those who triumphed in esports tournaments, appearing on an esports cable channel didn't change their lives a great deal.

With no route to professionalism, players suffered from a lack of stable income. The prize money, while nowhere close to present-day levels, was certainly appealing. But serious efforts to compete in tournaments required a degree of dedication that interfered with other daily obligations, affecting academic success. All for an uncertain windfall.

The gamer who tried to flunk school because they wanted to be the best player in history could expect a spanking from an angry parent. Even for those who reached the elite level, actually winning tournaments was far from guaranteed. There were many other excellent players out there. Another obstacle was the infrequency of tournaments. At first, there were only a few. With no dedicated training facilities or curriculum, the path to becoming an elite gamer was a rocky one.

Regardless of these hardships, some fanatics began to dream of becoming full-time gamers. And, as though God had listened to their entreaties, something miraculous happened.

CHAPTER 6

GOING PROFESSIONAL

Think back to your college years and imagine throwing a party.

Let's say you intend to host a casual, low-key party in your dorm room. You call up a few of your closest bros and dawgs to see if they are up for the idea. They are all up for it, so you stock the fridge with six-packs. You figure you'll hang out, maybe watch a ball game together. Some may show up as promised; some may not. It doesn't really matter. It's all good.

But then, without you realizing, the word spreads. Some of your bros casually share the info to other fellas and sistas. It turns out you're popular in your college community and beyond. News reaches neighboring colleges, where you are already well known to some people. News of the party spreads like wildfire. Many people you've never spoken to in your life decide to show up. Only one person—you—is unaware of what's about to go down.

On the day of the party, you expect a handful of close friends. Instead, thousands of people show up at your dorm. You don't know what the heck is going on, but you go with the flow. Somehow, you manage to throw an awesome impromptu party that is so great that everyone who attends still talks about it months later. Your party becomes a legend. Every year, to mark the occasion, you do it again.

Now imagine the same thing, except switching you and your dorm for an esports event in Busan, South Korea.

THE ESPORTS EVENT THAT CHANGED EVERYTHING

Back in 2004, two years after Korea and Japan jointly hosted the World Cup, esports exploded in Korea. The *StarCraft* League was sponsored by a Korean mobile phone provider called SKY, so the league was known as the Sky League. The organizer made a bold move and hosted the final championship outdoors, near a beach. At the time, almost all esports events took place in Seoul, but the organizer made a second bold move by locating the final in Busan, the second-largest city, on the south side of South Korea. Busan is about a six-hour drive from Seoul, the farthest city reachable by land transportation. The beach where the final was held is called Gwangalli Beach, one of the most famous beaches in Busan.

Unfortunately—or so it seemed—the Korean all-star professional baseball match was also scheduled to be held in Busan on the very same day. In Korea, baseball is easily the most popular spectator sport, followed by soccer.[1] Clearly, through bad luck or bad planning, the organizer of the Sky League had chosen a poor date for their event.

The Sajik Stadium, the baseball mecca where the all-star match was played, held thirty thousand people. Most people assumed that it would be packed to capacity, while the audience for the Sky League would be small. In fact, the Sajik stadium wasn't even close to capacity that day. The Sky League final championship, on the other hand, was packed with a whopping one hundred thousand people.[2]

It was a sensation. A hundred thousand people for an esports championship event! Nobody expected it. Many members of the audience came from outside Busan; some traveled all the way from Seoul. How large is a hundred-thousand-person-capacity stadium? The largest American football stadium by capacity is Michigan Stadium (at my alma mater), which holds just over one hundred thousand.

---

[1] Admittedly, this was shortly after the World Cup, so soccer was enjoying a spike in popularity.

[2] ["Gwangalli Battle," *Wikipedia*], https://ko.wikipedia.org/wiki/%EA%B4%91%EC%95%88%EB%A6%AC_%EB%8C%80%EC%B2%A9.

The 2019 Super Bowl, held at the Mercedes-Benz Stadium in Atlanta, Georgia, was attended by about seventy thousand people.

This episode changed everything. Big Korean companies, such as Samsung, took this indication of esports' popularity seriously enough to start sponsoring esports teams and players, accelerating the professionalization of the industry.

PROFESSIONAL TEAMS

HanbitSoft is a game publishing company that distributes *StarCraft* in South Korea. Naturally, the burgeoning popularity of esports led to a period of enormous success for the company. In addition, HanbitSoft also created probably the first-ever professional esports team. In hindsight, it made sense for the company that distributed *StarCraft* to sponsor a professional team, promoting the game and further boosting revenue. At a time when there was no such thing as a professional esports team, however, their move seemed audacious, to say the least.

Before professionalism, players relied on winning local tournaments to supplement their income. They practiced at local PC bangs, often striking a deal with the owners to bring in business. That quickly changed when esports went professional. Sponsors provided official contracts to the players, granting them an annual salary and a team-dedicated facility,[3] complete with gaming PCs and a bed. Suddenly, the players could present themselves as esports professionals, belonging to a team backed by a company like HanbitSoft.[4]

Soon after the birth of team HanbitSoft, other companies followed suit. SK Telecom, the largest telecommunication company in South Korea, launched a team called T1. T1 offered players the best salary and perks. Some earned six figures before bonuses or tournament prize money. Unlike other facilities, where practice rooms and accommodation were lumped together, T1's practice facilities and accommodation were separate. In-house caretakers took care of daily chores such as fixing meals, cleaning, and laundry, so players could focus on their gaming. During this period, T1 was always the strongest team in the league, roughly equivalent to Real Madrid in Spain's La Liga.

Another telecommunication company, Korea Telecom (KT) also launched a professional team, called KT Rolster. Because T1 and Rolster were both backed by giant telecommunication companies, and the teams fought it out at the top of the league, the match received a lot of attention. Sometimes it was referred to as the telecom derby. Tech conglomerate Samsung created Samsung Khan; CJ,

---

3 Usually an officetel—a cross between an office and a hotel—a common form of residence in South Korea.

4 Not everyone belonging to the team received a salary. Teams operated under a strict tier system and only the top-tier players were rewarded. Their positions were constantly challenged by lower-tier players.

the father company of esports cable channel OnGameNet, sponsored CJ Entus.

WHAT IT TAKES TO BE A PROFESSIONAL PLAYER

Being a good gamer could mean a few weekends of sleepless nights. But being a professional was another level entirely. Just like traditional sports, reaching a professional level takes constant practice and dedication.

I have never been a professional player, so I do not personally know the sacrifices it takes to reach that level. But a classmate of mine almost hit those heights. He was considered semi-pro. He was ridiculously good. The number of units he produced, the timing of his attacks, his overall tactics, and his micro-control of his units was on another level. For me, there was no chance of beating him. But he could not make it to the professional level.

Actions per minute (APM) is a statistic that measures the number of mouse clicks and keyboard commands that a person performs in a given minute. A normal *StarCraft* player makes, on average, around one hundred APM throughout the match. A professional peaks at around three hundred to five hundred APM, three to five times more commands than a normal player.[5]

---

[5] APM is often considered to be like the running speed for a soccer player. As a soccer player, being fast may give you advantages, but it is not a necessary condition. You can still be a professional soccer player even if you can't run one hundred meters in eleven seconds. Same with esports players.

According to a former professional player, APM must be combined with a good understanding of the game, high in-game situational awareness, quick decision-making, strong psychology, concentration, determination to win, and—most importantly—self-confidence.[6]

PROFESSIONAL PROCEDURES

Once players become professionals, they are no longer playing for fun. They are practicing to win. This entails a change of mindset. For team managers, finding people with this kind of dedication can be extremely challenging. This was especially true before the scene became mature enough for them to easily scout talent. At first, esports offered no minor amateur leagues or rookie draft system. But thanks to the online nature of esports games and the many local tournaments that took place, there were often rumors about good players. Team coaches were always on the lookout for good players in the wild, so they heard these rumors pretty quickly. Coaches who heard about a player of interest contacted the player and requested a friendly match, much like a judo master sparring with a pupil to assess the pupil's skill.[7]

---

6 조형근, e스포츠, 나를 위한 지식 플러스, (주)넥서스, 2017. [Jo Hyeong-geun, *E-sports, Knowledge for the Sake of the Nation* (Nexus, 2017).]

7 I was once told by an esports team coach that it was possible to sense a different aura from a game unit controlled by the best players. I laughed at it, but the coach was dead serious.

If the new kid on the block passed the test, they proceeded to interview. Interviews were mainly about figuring out how sociable the players were because team training houses were packed with other actual or aspiring professionals, and success in esports requires a team effort. Sometimes coaches placed hopefuls into mock full-day training situations with other team members at the training house, to assess their ability to communicate.

Gamers who passed all these tests were officially signed up as trainees. Teams operated a strict tier system, with the top-tier players participating in official tournament leagues while lower-tier players functioned as sparring opponents for the top-tier players until the latter climbed the ranks.

Team members lived in their team training houses, training as much as ten hours a day. They may once have become interested in gaming because it was an experience of entertainment and joy, but as professionals they were disciplined and dedicated. Just as in other highly competitive fields, many of them never made it to the professional ranks. Some tried for several years without ever reaching the top or attaining a proper salary.

THE PERKS OF BEING A PROFESSIONAL

Let's talk about the income of professional gamers.

A professional esports player belonging to a professional team receives a salary paid by the team, just like any person working a regular job. Those who demonstrate a good track record of winning may earn a raise for the following season.

On top of regular salaries, players are also incentivized to win tournament events. These incentives, while less than players would earn for winning a tournament independently, can be quite significant.[8] When *StarCraft* was booming, in the pre-smartphone era, media and event performances were another source of income. Professional gamers received invitations to perform at college festivals, a popular type of South Korean event, and attend autograph signings. In each case, players received a cut of the fee from broadcasters and/or event organizers.

Nowadays, online streaming channels have become an important source of income. Many professional players have a channel on streaming platforms such as YouTube and Twitch, where they broadcast live or recorded practice matches. Different streaming platforms offer different monetization options. Some channels operate a subscription model, in which the viewer pays the channel. The channel owner takes some of that income, the platform owner takes the rest. Other channels are free to watch. When they become sufficiently popular, channel owners

---

[8]   The 2018 *League of Legends* championship had a total prize pool of $6.45 million, whereas the *Dota 2* tournament offered prize money totaling $25.5 million.

receive compensation in exchange for allowing the platform to sell advertising space.

Another common form of streaming channel income is donations. Yes, you read that right—people *donate*, sometimes a hefty sum of cash, to watch others play video games. Donations are essentially rewards for awesome pieces of gameplay.[9]

KOREA E-SPORTS ASSOCIATION (KESPA)

In 1999, an official not-for-profit organization to promote esports was formed with the approval of the Korean government. This organization later became the Korea e-Sports Association (KeSPA).

KeSPA brought order to the somewhat chaotic world of esports. The organization's intention was first and foremost to improve the well-being of professional esports athletes. To do this, KeSPA provided standards and guidelines, an important shift. KeSPA-certified professional esports players received a reduction in income tax, from 22 percent down to 3.3 percent. Later, KeSPA started applying certification to both domestic and foreign game titles, tournament leagues, and PC bangs. For a game, tournament, or bang to be "KeSPA certified" was a mark of quality, similar to

---

9   Afreeca TV is a good example of such a business model in South Korea.

"Intel Inside" on a laptop. KeSPA supported approved tournaments with resources such as well-trained referees.

Most of the games used for esports tournaments in Korea, notably *StarCraft*, were published overseas. Without the agreement of Blizzard, the game's publisher, it would have been impossible to organize esports tournaments. Therefore, it was important that there was an entity that could negotiate with the holders of game rights. KeSPA naturally filled that role. In a way, KeSPA became a way for the Korean government to regulate what could otherwise have been a completely market-driven industry.[10] The organization has continued to thrive and KeSPA is now an official member of the Korean Olympic Committee and the International e-Sports Federation.

PROFESSIONAL SPORTS AND ESPORTS ATHLETES

A key difference between traditional sports and esports is that traditional sports work under the assumption that players have all the information they need to succeed. In soccer, for example, players know where the ball is, where all the other players are positioned, and in what formation. The same can be said of basketball. In mental games such

---

10 Organizations of this kind are never perfect. Some of KeSPA's activities—such as negotiating broadcasting rights with Blizzard, which I will touch upon in the following chapter—did cause controversy.

as chess and go, the board reveals exactly which moves players have made.

In esports, that is often not the case. Players of game genres like RTS, FPS, and MOBA work constantly with only partial information about their opponent's position. In *StarCraft*, for example, players only get information from the vicinity of their units, so if a unit does not see an opponent's unit, they have no information about the opponent's moves. Sometimes players don't even know where in the game an opponent is positioned without a search, and other players can always enact strategic location changes.

Working with partial information, professional esports athletes constantly seek out the latest information while hypothesizing what their opponent is doing. This requires lots of brainpower.

Just like athletes in other sports, esports athletes are vulnerable to injuries from long hours of sitting and never-ending micro-control movements of mouse and keyboard. Common forms of injury include carpal tunnel syndrome, herniated discs, and hemorrhoids.

DIRECTORS AND COACHES

For teams to function professionally, they need an operational structure. Each professional sports team has a director or a head coach, who leads the team and decides on strategy, along with a coach—or a group of specialized coaches—to guide individual players in the development of their skillset.

When esports became a serious business with committed corporate sponsorship, esports teams took a similar approach to their traditional counterparts. The team directors usually focused on external matters, such as securing external sources of sponsorship for the next season.

Esports coaches were often former professional players who understood the ins and outs of becoming a dedicated gamer. These coaches provided realistic feedback on players' day-to-day performance, leading toward future improvement. Coaches also set up practice matches for their teams, knowing that finding the right sparring opponent was quite challenging. Ideally, players should practice against people slightly better than them, a tough ask for the highest-ranked gamers.

OBSERVERS

RTS, FPS, and MOBA games only provide a first-person view of the action. For spectators who want to see the whole picture, this presents a conundrum. How can they watch the game? The answer is through an observer, a cameraman tasked with revealing the game situation as it progresses. These observers decide where to look and provide a third-person point of view of what's happening. Spectators, online or offline, see what the observer decides to look at.

Often, multiple actions are taking place at the same time, so the observer must decide what to show the audience. Sometimes this can be challenging. Game situations can change very quickly, and observers could completely miss the most important developments. If this happens—if an epic battle is happening, for instance, and the observer shows something unrelated—the audience will quickly lose interest. Imagine that LeBron James is about to score a dunk that will change the dynamics of the game, but the cameraman decides to show the coach sitting on the sidelines. It wouldn't make any sense.

Observers need to understand the games they observe, so former professional gamers often do the job.

REFEREES

Sometimes shit happens.

Imagine that, during a fierce match, your computer suddenly shows a blue screen, the keyboard stops functioning properly, or your mouse does something funky. What do you do? You call up the referee.

Being a competitive game with a lot at stake, esports requires a referee. The referee has the authority to pause the game in case of an emergency, or to stop it to adjudicate questions of cheating. If the game seems to be moving toward a draw, a rare situation in esports but not unheard of, the referee must decide whether to call it a draw. If so, it must be replayed, a considerable burden to players who have already been under stress for hours. The referee also records data from each match, for example, by updating win-lose scoreboards.

In 2010, at a *StarCraft* League final in Korea, two legendary players were engaged in what could have become an everlasting classic. Suddenly, a blackout occurred.[11] Everyone in the venue, including the players and casters, was uncertain what to do. The referee had to make the tough call to abandon the game and move on to the next match.

WHY PEOPLE WATCH ESPORTS TOURNAMENTS OFFLINE

The above explains why esports can be highly entertaining, but it doesn't explain why one hundred thousand spectators would gather to watch an esports match in person. The answer is that offline esports events are extremely entertaining.

The overall atmosphere of these events is similar to profes-

---

11   Check it out yourself: https://youtu.be/HzVMUkSg17A

sional sports such as soccer or basketball. A large number of people show up at a stadium to root for their favorite team. Some wear team jerseys; some clap using the pair of long balloons you've surely seen if you've ever attended a live sports event. Spectators may not hear the commentary as clearly as they would at home or on a personal mobile device, but they may see what happens between shots.

Another perk of attending esports matches in person is seeing star players from as little as a few feet away. Attendees may get autographs, snap photos with their heroes, or even form friendships with other gamers. In between games, there is entertainment, such as performances by popular bands and cosplay exhibitions.

This kind of offline esports culture did not emerge fully formed. It grew for years under the radar. In the heart of Seoul, there is a large underground mall beneath Samsung station, which served as a public viewing space for the first offline tournament events. The space, known as Samsung Megabox Station, was located within a cineplex called Megabox. It was a perfect location for people who had some leisure time to kill before their movie started. Movie patrons could purchase popcorn and soda, then take a seat at Megabox Station and watch a *StarCraft* match between two professional gamers. The space also housed camera setups for channels like OnGameNet.

Even those with little prior interest in competitive gaming found this public viewing arena quite entertaining. Day by day, more people gathered. Soon, they started coming specifically to watch esports matches.

The growing esports fan base led to further changes as the industry grew and people began to take it more seriously. This increasing, unignorable popularity naturally led to higher-quality entertainment content and arguably the most glorious era in the history of Korean esports.

CHAPTER 7

THE RENAISSANCE OF SOUTH KOREAN ESPORTS

If the Renaissance in fifteenth-century Europe was an era that enabled humanity to reach another intellectual level, leading to breakthroughs in art and science, the 2000s was the renaissance of Korean esports. It was during this decade that the industry truly bloomed, following its early years of promise tempered with instability.

Following the 2004 *StarCraft* League finals that attracted over one hundred thousand fans to Busan, perceptions of esports shifted. Suddenly, being a professional esports athlete was not shameful—quite the opposite. People, especially young people, wanted to be professional esports players. The fame, the salary, and the perks, coupled with the fantasy of avoiding daily studies and playing games all day long, made becoming an esports professional seem like a dream career.

Not every esports fan is an avid gamer. Even for non-gamers, the competitions are entertaining to watch. At first sight, *StarCraft* might seem complicated, even intimidating, to those who have never played it, particularly if they have limited experience of other video games. But in fact, *StarCraft* is easy to understand, even without any relevant background. After watching a few rounds, people quickly get a sense of what is happening.

A complete *StarCraft* novice can encounter a match on OnGameNet, begin watching it out of curiosity, and soon become hooked. With the help of explanation from casters and commentators, and the adrenaline boost of their occasional screams and roars, the newcomer may soon develop an interest in watching esports and become a fan.

Following the incredible success of the *StarCraft* League finals in Busan, the industry went into a virtuous spiral. It quickly attracted more spectators, more sponsors, more tournament organizers, more pro teams, and more pro players, all playing for larger stakes.

At the epicenter of this virtuous spiral was the fierce competition between the professional players, who practiced day and night. The main content consumed by the fans was the epic duel between two brilliant players. Like gladiatorial combat in the Roman Colosseum centuries ago, bouts of *StarCraft* made for a great spectator sport. For the players, the stakes felt almost as high.

Players with strong track records rose in the rankings and gained more fans, especially if there was something original about them that endeared them to fans. Those who reached those rarefied heights became star players.

THE STAR PLAYERS

In my elementary school days in the early 1990s, I used to collect NBA cards. Michael Jordan, Scottie Pippen, Dennis Rodman (before he went a little weird politically), Grant Hill, Hakeem Olajuwon, David Robinson, Jason Kidd, John Stockton, Charles Barkley, Magic Johnson, Penny Hardaway (did I get the name right?), Gary Payton, Patrick Ewing, etc. Even though I don't follow the NBA at all nowadays, I can still remember these star players off the top of my head. I had strong emotional associations with the NBA, so it became part of my permanent memory.

The *StarCraft* professional league in the 2000s was similar to my favorite period of the NBA. I could still list at least as many esports star players as NBA stars, but because you're probably not familiar with them, I'll restrict myself to a few and explain what made them so successful.

LIM YO HWAN

This list of star players should begin with the best of all time. Lim Yo Hwan, frequently known by his player ID, SlayerS_'-BoxeR'. Mr. Lim was a Terran user who was perhaps the very first player to attain long-lasting stardom in *StarCraft* League. He is the Roger Federer of esports. A little older than the average player, Mr. Lim's play was creative and original. He defied typical strategies and tactics, instead creating his own. Fans called him the Terran Emperor. Aside from his brains and creativity, he clearly enjoyed video games in general, which fans appreciated. Thanks to his good looks, he attracted many female fans to a male-dominated market.

HONG JIN-HO

Korean fans will always remember one of Mr. Lim's great rivals, Hong Jin-Ho, also known as [NC]...YellOw. Mr. Hong is a Zerg user who competed in the same era as the BoxeR. His playing style was to storm his opponent with constant attacks, leading to the nickname "Storm Zerg." It wasn't his only nickname. Due to his rivalry with Mr. Lim, a rivalry in which he usually came second, Mr. Hong is known as "the Number Two."[1]

---

[1] He always made it to the finals but finished in second place, mostly to Mr. Lim. Koreans can be quite brutal in our choice of nickname, but this guy was a real man and embraced it. The nickname Number Two became his brand and character to the public. He owned the label in such a positive way that he gave the impression it was okay to be number two.

LEE YUN YEOL

When he debuted as a pro, Lee Yun Yeol, also known as NaDa, was one of the youngest players in the league. Despite his relative inexperience, he played like a veteran, shocking fans with his ability to produce units. It was always entertaining to watch him send a platoon of siege tanks toward his opponent's base, knowing that in a few seconds they would feel the force of his attack. Sometimes watching him even gave me chills. Mr. Lee has won many championships throughout his career.

FOREIGN STAR PLAYERS

You might imagine that the league was completely domestic, but that's not the case. Some foreign players attained the same level of stardom as Korean players. Guillaume Patry was a French-Canadian Protoss user who eventually triumphed in a *StarCraft* League. He invented many tactics that later became the standard for Protoss users. He too was a good-looking fella.

Bertrand Grospellier was a French Terran player with a lot of style. He *always* showed up wearing a pair of shades.[2] Impressively, he simultaneously played two different titles

---

[2] Rumor has it that nobody saw his naked eyes. Another tic he exhibited was holding a match in his mouth, like a character in a classic Wild West movie.

of RTS game professionally, roughly equivalent to playing two sports professionally.[3]

FUNNY EPISODES

Like any other event organized by humans, the professional *StarCraft* League threw up some funny moments that gave the fans unexpected additional entertainment. In this section, I'll share a few of my favorites.

THE HEADPHONE EPISODE

Casters and commentators are human beings too. We have all seen news anchors burst into laughter during a live broadcast, due to some surprising event. I would say that the casters and commentators of the esports league experienced such incidents more frequently. On the bright side, fans watched the channel for entertainment anyway, so these interludes enhanced the action as opposed to detracting from it.

One such episode was caused by a professional player who mistakenly wore his headphones completely inside-out, with the speakers facing outwards. The poor guy didn't even notice his mistake.

---

[3] He often reached the semi-finals of *StarCraft* Leagues and also sometimes reached the grand finals of *Warcraft III*. He must have some kind of dual-core processor in his brain.

The caster and the commentator switched their audio to silent to avoid betraying their mirth, but anyone watching video of the incident can see that they are trying very hard not to burst into tears of laughter. As the awkward silence continues, one commentator with more self-control than the others realizes that the situation could head south and exhorts his fellow commentators, "Bros, you gotta chill out." This incident became a legendary episode in Korean esports broadcasting.[4]

VICTORY CELEBRATIONS

Just as a soccer player scoring a goal might perform a victory celebration in front of their fans, some *StarCraft* players did the same. This was rare at first, because celebrations after winning a match were usually relatively reserved, for example, high fives. Some players, such as Lee Sung Eun, broke out of this mold, intentionally performing elaborate celebrations directly in front of freshly defeated opponents. It must have been a bitter pill for the defeated opponents, but for the fans it was highly entertaining.[5]

GIRLS IN THE ESPORTS SCENE

The star players attracted not only fanatical boys but also girls to the esports scene. Until esports became hugely

---

[4] Please watch it yourself: https://youtu.be/V8nmsHY2QPA

[5] A clip is here: https://youtu.be/-RCPwCuc268

popular, girls in South Korea showed little interest in the gaming market. Few girls owned game consoles or admitted to playing games.[6]

The game arcades were even worse. They were completely restricted to males, like strict Turkish teahouses in the conservative eastern region of the country. This was probably partly due to the environment of the arcades.[7] When the businesses embraced franchising, arcades became brighter and cleaner, improving their overall atmosphere. They also moved to more welcoming locations, for example, next to movie theaters.

During the Korean renaissance era, esports began to attract girls to the scene as well. As a rule, however, the girls were less attracted by the contents of the games and more enticed by the star players. Some of these star players had good looks that resonated well with young Korean girls, even if they had no other interest in the games.

Around this time, K-pop bands such as Super Junior, Big Bang, and TVXQ were formed to appeal to a similar market. Female Korean teenagers happily spent their money on fan

---

[6] During my pre-college years in Korea, I only met two girls who were into gaming. Maybe Korean society was too conservative at the time.

[7] The typical arcade was dark and run-down, even during daylight hours. Fights sometimes broke out over whether someone was cheating. They weren't places girls wanted to hang out.

merchandise, and many of these bands later enjoyed worldwide commercial success.

Ironically, the teenage girls who initially seemed to be uninterested in games ultimately had a big influence on the South Korean esports scene. Male fans were mainly interested in playing games and less likely to purchase merchandise. Female fans, on the other hand, showed up to every match their favorite gamer played, often with handmade placards. They were quite happy to spend money on goods associated with the players they loved.[8]

Another way in which girls got involved in the esports scene was through dates. Not the most romantic dates, but dates nonetheless. Allow me to explain. We've established that Korean guys love hanging out in PC bangs with their bros. But some guys were in relationships when the esports scene exploded. They were expected to take their significant others to romantic venues, such as restaurants, movies, or amusement parks.

This happened at the beginning of the relationship, but soon the guys reverted to playing games in PC bangs, ignoring text messages and phone calls from their girlfriends. They weren't being deliberately mean; they were just distracted.

---

[8] OnGameNet always broadcasted footage of the audience before the match began, and the numbers of schoolgirls in uniform rapidly increased. They never liked showing their faces on camera and always covered them with their placards immediately after they realized they were being filmed.

This resulted in angry girlfriends who came to see PC bangs as rivals for their boyfriend's attention.

Some of these guys had an idea to defuse the conflict. They took their girlfriends on PC bang dates. They persuaded their girlfriends to join them at the PC bangs, where they could sit next to each other. He played *StarCraft*; she spent hours watching her favorite drama on the internet. A cost-effective way to mollify angry girlfriends.[9]

Fast-forward a few months and the girlfriend who has spent hours in a PC bang knows all the rules of *StarCraft*, either from watching or from getting curious and playing the game herself. Imagine this situation replicated throughout South Korea, and you'll recognize a system that produces *StarCraft*-friendly females at scale.

As the population of interested females grew, there was enough interest to start a female pro league.

FEMALE PRO LEAGUE AND STAR PLAYERS

During the hottest era of *StarCraft* League, the main league was dominated by male players, but there was enough interest to accommodate a female-only pro league. Just

---

[9] Some girls complained that they didn't like the smoky smell or dark atmosphere of PC bangs, but there were more than twenty thousand nationwide. It was always possible to find a cleaner, brighter one.

like the men, there were female star players with skills and charisma to spare. I'll describe two of the most memorable.

SEO JI-SOO

Seo Ji-Soo, user ID ToSsGirL, is a Terran user who attracted much attention. She was good. Really good.[10] On top of her performance, she had a distinguished beautiful look, reminiscent of a TV celebrity. Male gamers who watched her play found it hard to resist becoming her fanboy. Even guys who weren't into games were attracted by her looks. Not many people are both competent esports professionals and highly attractive. She managed both.

KIM GA EUL

Kim Ga Eul, user ID [Oops]January, was another distinguished star player in the female league. She was known for her high level of play, which was as good as a male professional. Her style was extremely intelligent, and some fans believed she was making full use of her engineering background.[11] Although her playing career was successful, her real success came later, as I will explain in a future chapter.

---

10 I recently met a professional Korean esports coach who used to play matches with ToSsGirL and who held her in awe. In his eyes, she was the only female player who could match male professionals. Without intending to sound discriminatory, male versus female *StarCraft* matches were like male versus female basketball games: there was a clear gap in the standards of game play. ToSsGirL was the only female player who could compete in the male professional league.

11 Female engineering students were quite rare in Korea at the time.

ESPORTS IN THE MILITARY

Due to the unique situation between North and South Korea, South Korean males are required to serve in the army. This is mandatory for all male South Korean citizens unless they have a serious, chronic medical issue. Military service involves spending about two years completely shut off from modern civilization during the most energetic time of their lives, normally between the ages of nineteen and twenty-five.

Professional esports players were subject to the same fate as any other Korean male citizens, but mandatory military duty represented a particularly serious problem for their careers. Why? The esports scene is extremely competitive. Most players made their debuts as teenagers. By their twenties, their physical reaction times were already beginning to deteriorate. The average *StarCraft* professional should have a retirement plan in place by the time he reaches his mid- to late twenties.[12] For a professional esports player, two years in the military was more or less the death knell for his career.

How was this situation resolved? The Korean government launched a special force for esports professionals. From 2006, a professional esports team was formulated under the Korean Air Force. It was named ACE, an acronym meaning Airforce Challenges E-sports. The name might

---
12 It's a career arc similar to the professional figure skating scene.

be cheesy, but it was an oasis for many esports professionals hoping to continue their careers.

Of course, not every esports player could be part of this squad, only carefully selected players with track records and vigor. Once they became part of this team, the players underwent six weeks of base-camp training stationed in the countryside of South Korea, in a humble Air Force base. In many ways they were like normal trainees, who had no access to computers at all. The difference is that, after completing their six-week training, professional esports players were permitted to continue practicing *StarCraft* as a team, as their main daily "military" duty.

Occasionally, they were allowed to go to Seoul to participate in *StarCraft* tournament events; they often toured military bases demonstrating their skills at local esports events. Compared to the routines of a regular cadet, which consisted of dull duties such as cleaning guns and preparing meals, esports professionals were extremely privileged. Many of the scene's star players spent their military service with ACE.

ESPORTS PLAYERS ON REGULAR TV

The star player Mr. Lim (AKA SlayerS_`BoxeR`) was respected in the esports community not simply because he played well, but also because he did a good job of reaching out to the wider community. He was a great advocate for esports and appeared on national television to describe the life of a professional esports player.

At the time, this was a big deal. There was no precedent for esports professionals appearing on national television with a long enough airtime. His first appearance, however, revealed the prejudices of Korean society at the time. The broadcasters introduced Mr. Lim as an esports professional but portrayed him as a game addict. He was a legendary esports player, leading the Korean esports renaissance, but he was introduced as a game addict without a decent job! It was a public humiliation.

Despite this initial humiliation, his bravery in appearing on national TV introduced a whole new audience to esports. Many laypeople learned what esports is and understood that being an esports athlete could be a full-time job. More youngsters with big dreams joined the esports crusade, and a more established generation began to respect the industry.

THE AIR JORDAN OF ESPORTS

I used to be obsessed with Nike sneakers. My mom wouldn't buy them for me because they were more expensive than other brands, so I never got a pair of Nikes until I was in high school. Thanks to that memory, I still have a thing for

Nike sneakers, even in my mid-thirties. I have a few pairs of Air Jordans now and I just love 'em.

As you probably know, Air Jordan is a signature Nike brand that became famous when Michael Jordan wore them during his legendary career in the nineties. NBA players don't have a lot of say in the design of their uniforms, but they can express their individuality through their choice of shoes. As an active sport, basketball also requires quality footwear. A player's choice of shoes influences their performance, especially at the highest level. Only the very best players, such as Michael Jordan, qualify for a signature brand.

The same is true of esports. For PC games like *StarCraft*, a mouse and keyboard is to a professional esports player what a pair of shoes is to a professional basketball player. After trying out hundreds of different brands, a player will be thoroughly attached to his favorite mouse and keyboard by the time he reaches professional status. To an experienced esports player, any subtle difference in the click or the touch sound can affect his game. Computer hardware manufacturers collaborate with top players and teams to create signature mouse and keyboard models.[13]

---

13 If your game-loving son or daughter owns a slightly more expensive mouse and keyboard than a bundle, the chances are they may be using a signature model.

WORLD CYBER GAMES AND INTERNATIONALIZING

In 2000, an event styled as the Olympics of esports was born under the sponsorship of the South Korean government and Samsung. The event was called the World Cyber Games (WCG) and the first main event was held in 2001. After that, it was held on an annual basis, first in South Korea, and then in various locations around the globe, including the United States, Singapore, Italy, Germany, and China.

WCG gradually attracted more participating national teams and became a great success. From seventeen countries in 2000, the event featured seventy-eight at its peak. The involvement of giant sponsors such as Samsung and Microsoft—the event was a perfect showcase for new Windows and Xbox products—increased the total prize pool. Competitors played the most popular esports games, such as *StarCraft*, *Quake*, and *FIFA*, with medals and cash prizes up for grabs.[14] This also made WCG an important channel for game publishers to promote new titles.

The main appeal, however, were the tournament events. WCG was probably the first esports competition that allowed gamers to compete as national teams. Korean esports professionals represented the Republic of Korea and competed against the representatives of other countries.

---

14   Not every game title was featured; only those that passed a popularity vote a year after their release.

The South Korean team was among the top-ranked in WCG in every game, but for *StarCraft*, they were invincible. The Korean national team won gold medals in *StarCraft* for fourteen consecutive years, starting from 2000.[15]

Through WCG, the gaming world began to take South Korean gaming seriously. Eventually, Koreans earned the reputation of being born with *StarCraft* DNA in their genes.

THE END OF THE RENAISSANCE

The European Renaissance in the fifteenth century lasted more than two hundred years. Unfortunately, the esports renaissance in South Korea lasted slightly less than a decade.

Some may argue that less than a decade in the internet age is equivalent to a couple of centuries in fifteenth-century Europe, but that's beyond the scope of this book. What is more important is *why* the renaissance came to an end.

The downhill story begins with a match-fixing scandal.

---

[15] It is like the United States national basketball team, which has won Olympic gold almost every game since 1992, in Barcelona (when it was known as the Dream Team), with the notable exception of 2004 in Athens. Some years, the Korean team won all three medals in *StarCraft*.

CHAPTER 8

A PARTY POOPER

In 2010, it was alleged that a professional *StarCraft* player was conspiring to fix matches in one of the major *StarCraft* leagues. Unfortunately, the player was one of the game's legends, with the skills, track record, and looks to attract a huge fan base. He was renowned for pioneering a new strategy within the game that many players found thought-provoking, a strategy that soon became the standard build-order. He won many official tournaments and was highly ranked in the overall prize standings.

A few days later, the allegation turned out to be true. The Korean esports industry went into shock. It was as though Roger Federer had been caught cheating at tennis, Cristiano Ronaldo at soccer, or LeBron James at basketball. All the credibility the player had earned by winning a series of tournament matches was suddenly in question.

The South Korean Supreme Prosecutors' Office investigated further, and it soon became clear that the fixed game wasn't a one-off. It was part of a bigger plan, executed by the player, other esports professionals, a soccer player from the K-League (South Korea's professional soccer league), and a Korean mobster. In short, the scale of the alleged misconduct was larger than it had first looked. It was well coordinated and carefully planned.

After the Prosecutors' Office announced its investigation, the South Korean news media took the incident very seriously. All three major national TV channels reported on it. This was unusual. As a rule, news shows rarely report on esports, and when they do it's normally relegated to the sports section of the broadcast. Unfortunately, given the seriousness and scale of the scandal, the match-fixing news made headlines. This also meant that for many people unfamiliar with esports, their first impression of the scene was associated with scandal.

THE AFTERMATH OF THE SCANDAL

After weeks of investigation and months of litigation, the people involved in the match-fixing scandal were appropriately punished. The player at the center of the wrongdoing was sentenced to a year of imprisonment, a couple of years of probation, and 120 hours of social services, which he faithfully completed. His professional contract was immediately terminated, and he was permanently banned from the esports professional leagues by KeSPA.

I wish this was the end of this unfortunate episode in Korean esports history. But unfortunately, it was not. When the national news media reported an esports scandal, it attracted the attention of many decision-makers, both inside and outside of the industry. Soon, many sponsors of esports started to get cold feet. The following season, hardly any big-name companies were willing to start or continue sponsoring esports. From a corporate standpoint, this was understandable. Brands considered esports mainly as a marketing channel for their brands, but after the scandal, the sport projected an image they no longer wished to be associated with.

Some key elements of the esports scene, such as professional teams and tournament leagues, rely on sponsorship income. Losing sponsors threatened their very existence. Consequently, about half of the professional teams that existed prior to the scandal were dismantled. Major esports tournament leagues either shut down or significantly downsized.

Worse, Korean esports also lost many fans, disgusted by the betrayal of one of their heroes. Dwindling sponsorship and fan base affected another critical aspect of the esports industry: broadcasting. At the time, there were two dedicated esports cable channels. OnGameNet survived. The other did not.

Once the symbol of a successful esports career, the ACE team owned and run by the Korean Air Force was discontinued. Since then, undertaking military service has meant an immediate end to the professional career of an esports player.

Due to the match-fixing scandal, the renaissance era of esports came to an end. Thousands of esports professionals were laid off: players, event organizers, casters, and commentators. The esports industry no longer seemed like a viable employment option.

MORE SCANDAL

Just as the esports world was reeling from one scandal, it was beset by others. Throughout the following years, the South Korean esports scene suffered from various match-fixing scandals, although none were as major as the first. The esports scene was like a person constantly catching a mild cold, regardless of the season. A little cough here and there did not prevent the esports scene from moving forward, but it was certainly bothersome.

Just as a cough can develop into pneumonia, so minor scandals can develop into major ones. In 2015, the esports scene was rocked by another major match-fixing scandal, as well organized as the one in 2010. Unfortunately, the fixing took place in a *StarCraft II* league, further tainting the game that led the South Korean esports renaissance.

BROADCASTING RIGHTS DISPUTES

One key way in which esports differs from traditional sports is in who owns the rights.[1] Sport itself is not owned by any entity: soccer is not owned by FIFA, its international governing body. In other words, you don't have to pay FIFA, or any other entity, to play soccer at your local field. Esports is different. The core game content is owned by a game publisher, which is a for-profit corporation, and that ownership is secured by copyright or intellectual property (IP). If I want to play a video game, I need to compensate the game publisher accordingly. This led to another incident that made an impact on the Korean esports scene.

A common business model in the video gaming world is paying for the rights to play.[2] If I purchase a piece of game software—say, *Super Mario Bros.*—I can play it

---

[1] I do not intend to describe in detail the legal conflict I am about to discuss, because like any legal conflict, it is complicated. I don't want to risk taking sides on an issue with which I was not directly involved.

[2] Nowadays, this business model is less common. Most publishers allow people to play games free of charge. Anyone can download and install them. Publishers earn money from in-game user purchases, such as items and skins.

whenever I want. Alternatively, I can go to the arcade, insert a quarter in a *Pac-Man* machine, and play until my credit runs out. Prior to the success of esports, *StarCraft* followed a similar model. Anyone could buy a copy of *StarCraft*, install it on their machine, and play as much as they liked.

Now let's say I throw a private game-night party at home, using a video game I have purchased. I design the party in a tournament format. The party is so successful that people are willing to pay a few bucks to watch the tournament participants show off their skills. As host, I end up making a little profit from my tournament by selling tickets to spectators. Now imagine something similar happening, but on a much larger, national scale, where the party host is KeSPA, the Korean e-Sports Association.[3]

For traditional sports such as soccer, this doesn't represent a problem. For specific game titles, created and owned by game publishers, it does. No doubt the publishers of *StarCraft* were delighted to see their game at the epicenter of a national esports boom, but they weren't happy to see an unauthorized third party profiting from their IP.

As a result, KeSPA and the game's publisher entered into a protracted legal dispute. The dispute ended sourly, with

---

[3] To be precise, KeSPA did not sell tickets to spectators. Instead, the organization sold broadcasting rights to esports channels like OnGameNet.

both *StarCraft* and *StarCraft II* leagues in Korea eventually terminated indefinitely.[4]

A LEGENDARY COMMENTATOR FALLS FROM GRACE

The decline of esports had an impact on people throughout the profession. For one famous commentator who played a major role in turning esports commentary into an accepted profession, life took a particularly sour turn. It's difficult to isolate cause and effect, but a combination of reduced demand and his underperformance as a commentator led to his ostracization from the esports scene.

After he disappeared from official tournaments and broadcasting channels, he started to appear on online channels such as YouTube and its South Korean equivalent. Then he disappeared again. His next public appearance came in a completely different context. His name was on a flyer for a local night business. Yes, he had become a pimp.

The esports fans of the renaissance era, by this time in their thirties and forties, had watched esports rise from the status of a dodgy subculture to mainstream entertainment. They were furious with their former hero for bringing the scene into disrepute and for leveraging the nostalgia

---

4 Unlike traditional sports, an individual game has a limited life span. No matter how popular the game, sooner or later it is replaced by another. In my opinion, the *StarCraft* League lasted longer than anybody could have expected. The *StarCraft II* League, meanwhile, ended sooner than it might have done.

of esports fans to promote his night business. In any case, his new incarnation didn't last long. He soon disappeared again, his career in the adult entertainment industry over.[5]

OTHER ESPORTS ISSUES

Unlike traditional sports, which occur face-to-face, gamers can anonymize their background and personal information behind a username or an avatar. This means that there's potential for rude and hurtful behavior to occur. To an extent, taunting an opposing player is accepted in both traditional sports and esports,[6] but some people in the esports world take it to an extreme. It is not uncommon for gamers to come up against opposing players who deliver serious insults via text and voice during the game. While some people object to this practice, others claim that it's just part of video gaming.

Another issue in the esports world is the existence of third-party software programs that help players to win. For RTS games, for instance, players can use a software program called MapHack that allows the player to see what their opponent is doing in real time. It's like being able to see

---

[5] I don't know what he does for a living now, but he has disappeared from the mainstream. I am sure the passage after the esports commentator career must have been very difficult for him. Sometimes I wonder what would have happened if the esports renaissance era had continued. It seems sad and unnecessary for a legendary former commentator to have found himself working at an adult night business.

[6] Except for an exceptional case like Marco Materazzi of Italy seriously insulting Zinedine Zidane of France in the 2006 World Cup Final, to which Zidane responded with a headbutt.

other players' hands during a game of poker. For FPS games, a program called FPSHelper improves the player's aim during the game. Imagine wearing an Iron Man suit that does all your aiming automatically, and you'll have an idea of how this program affects gaming. These software programs are all against the fair play of esports.

AN INDUSTRY IN NEED OF GOVERNANCE AND COMPLIANCE

Let's consider the match-fixing scandal again. Who is to blame?

Does all the blame for the wrongdoing fall on the one influential player who committed the initial crime? If the fall of the Korean esports scene is entirely due to one person, how do we explain other scandals, such as the second major match-fixing scandal in 2015?

In hindsight, I think it was a matter of time before a similar scandal occurred. The Korean esports industry as a whole must take as much responsibility as the individual concerned. As a new and quickly changing industry, esports lacked consistent standards. To an extent, that's still the case. For corporate enterprises, auditing has become an internationally expected way to maintain quality, prolong healthy business activities, and reassure stakeholders. Esports at the time of the scandal had no similar quality-assurance protocol.

The industry lacked a form of governance and compliance that would have regulated it effectively. It was heavily focused on growth, with much less attention given to activities that could have protected esports from damage to its reputation. There was no watchdog or whistleblower.

If the industry had been proactive about establishing systematic safeguards to prevent cheating, perhaps the likelihood of such a scandal could have been reduced. At the very least, a strong system of governance and compliance could have provided early warnings to industry stakeholders before the entire industry was shaken and thousands of people lost their jobs.[7]

To this day, esports governance and compliance is not close to the level of corporate auditing. The good news, however, is that the industry is making an effort to improve. Since the industry-shaking scandal, for example, KeSPA has institutionalized a mandatory education program on player ethics that esports professionals must take regularly to maintain their license.

PLAYING IN A BOOTH

Esports can offer some cases of successfully implementing rules and regulations. One of them is the use of a sound-

---

[7] This is one of the reasons why I have started an esports advisory group at a Big Four auditing firm.

proof booth, similar to the ones used by musicians or real-time interpreters.

Why? In the early days of the esports league, when rules and regulations were still informal, players used to share the same space as the audience. The players did wear headsets, but some sound could still sneak through. With casters and commentators speaking constantly, and an audience sometimes screaming for their team, live esports can get pretty noisy.

When esports spectators watch a pivotal moment in the game unfold,[8] they get agitated and start to scream and yell, as do the casters and commentators. Sometimes, players heard the crowd's reaction, and some of the cleverer ones gauged what was about to happen from the audience reaction. This led them to change their tactics and make different moves, potentially influencing the outcome of the match.[9]

Realizing this risk, event organizers instigated a rule mandating that players play in a completely soundproof gaming booth.

---

8 Such as a group of stop lurkers waiting for an opponent's marines and medics to pass.

9 Korean fans used to call this phenomenon an "ear map."

LEGISLATION: CINDERELLA'S LAW

Many parents worry that their children will become addicted to games and play them all night long. In fairness, some do. This concern has led to a change in the law. Since 2011, children below the age of sixteen have been banned from accessing online games between 12 a.m. and 6 a.m., a regulation known as Cinderella's Law.[10] This law can be enforced because many online games in Korea require users to input their date of birth.

When Cinderella's Law came into force, it caused many ripples in the Korean esports community. The community reacted furiously, claiming that this new regulation must have been created by politicians who understood little about the gaming community.

Many wannabe professionals start training hard before they reach the age of sixteen, and many heavy gamers are nocturnal by nature, so stakeholders were concerned that the regulation would directly interfere with the development of talented gamers.

From a practical point of view, people below the age of sixteen can easily sidestep the law by providing one of their parents' date of birth, but game publishers have a legal responsibility to enforce it. Thailand adopted a similar

---

10   A violation of the regulation by the game publisher/provider may result in a maximum of two years of imprisonment or a fine of no more than 10 million KRW (about 10,000 USD).

rule in 2003 but abandoned it after two years of trial for the reasons described above. In Korea, Cinderella's Law is still in effect to this day.

A PART OF KOREAN SOCIETY

South Korea has seen a majestic period of esports prosperity, which many of us still view as the renaissance of esports. Yet the country has also experienced the bursting of that bubble, shaking an industry that seemed as though it could continue growing indefinitely. This downturn cost the industry dearly, with many stakeholders losing businesses and jobs. Imagine eating an exquisite meal at a fancy restaurant, only to have it ruined by a disastrous dessert.

Despite this bitter experience, the South Korean esports saga hasn't come to an end. We have all seen bubbles inflate, then burst, many with painful effects on the people who invested in them. The subprime mortgage crash that shook the global economy in 2008. The bursting of the dotcom bubble in the early 2000s. Going back even further, the optimism of the nineteenth-century gold rush came to a sudden and ignominious end. The bursting of the South Korean esports bubble has cost a lot of jobs, but it hasn't been terminal.

Since its birth circa 1999, esports has been part of Korean society for more than two decades. Those two decades, including both positive and negative experiences, have only deepened the affection of Koreans toward esports.

Not every burst bubble is a disaster. Since the dotcom crash, businesses based on the internet have matured, leading to new markets and many new forms of business. Without the internet, we wouldn't have smartphones. Sometimes the popping of a bubble can represent a necessary correction. This may well be the case with the esports industry in South Korea, which now seems to be moving in the right direction. Just as the internet has now assumed a central role in human society, so the role of esports in Korean society continues to grow.

In the final chapter of this book, we'll explore this phenomenon.

CHAPTER 9

SOCIETAL INTEGRATION

Did the esports scene in Korea stop after the party-pooping incidents? No. It matured.

The number of PC bangs in Korea, which peaked at more than twenty thousand around the year 2000, has now halved. This is because the market has matured and moved toward a franchise model, with small, independent businesses consolidating into larger chains. When I enthusiastically visited PC bangs in the late nineties, most were small, housing around fifty PCs. Back then, it was hard to find a facility with more than a hundred PCs.

Since those days, the small- to medium-sized enterprises have mostly died out, replaced by large franchises offering hundreds of PCs and impeccable service. There may be fewer PC bangs overall, but they can still be found almost anywhere in South Korea.

Speaking of service, modern-day PC bangs have taken it to another level. These large facilities contain the highest-spec gaming PCs, each one equipped with thin, curved monitors that don't tire the eyes, even after long hours of staring at a screen. Each PC is paired with a comfy esports chair with an ergonomic design to accommodate long hours of sitting, worth more than $1,500, and a high-quality headset. Most people don't own such a top-notch set of gaming gear, so the chance to use the highest-quality kit on the market has become another reason to visit a PC bang.

The overall interior design of these PC bangs is slick and clean, a world away from the dingy styles of the late nineties. Female customers, who tend to be more sensitive to their environment, have become regular customers. Some PC bangs also have designated couples' areas, where normal seats are replaced by comfy two-seater sofas, judiciously placed in front of two gaming PCs so that a couple can combine gaming and cuddling.

Pricing at PC bangs has changed little from the early days. It's usually calculated on a pay-to-play basis and is no more expensive than it was twenty years ago. In the nineties, the standard cost was about two to three dollars per hour; nowadays it is around one to two dollars, which is insanely cost-efficient considering the increase in the cost of living in Korea over the past two decades.

You may wonder how PC bang owners turn a profit. The answer is that they provide additional services, such as food and beverages. Many franchised PC bangs now offer a decent food menu, prepared at a dedicated on-site kitchen. The average menu features everything from burgers and fries to common Korean daily dishes such as kimchi fried rice and *tteokbokki*. Ramen noodles are still available, albeit much higher-quality versions than the cup noodles offered in the first PC bangs.

Some bangs even have a decent Italian espresso coffee machine, similar to the ones used at restaurants, with dedicated in-house baristas to make lattes for gamers. Customers order from an electronic menu, directly from their computer, and a waiter or waitress delivers the food and beverages. PC bangs are still open 24/7 all year long, and some start to sell alcoholic drinks after midnight.

PC BANG CULTURE FOR EVERYONE

Given the ubiquity of the facilities, the cost-effectiveness of the service they provide, and their longevity, PC bangs are now more than simply a business. They have become an established part of Korean culture. In Korea, everyone from the most senior vice president to the most junior employee is acquainted with *StarCraft* and PC bangs. At corporate social events, it's common for game-playing to act as a way of breaking down social barriers.

After work, it's common for colleagues in Korea to go to PC bangs together. Even more common is for coworkers to have a few drinks, then top off the evening with a trip to a PC bang, as an alternative to the stereotypical Korean evening of sinking epic quantities of *soju*[1] and turning the night into a big party. Some younger people in their twenties prefer not to drink heavily, so this more low-key approach to a night out has become the status quo in some workplaces.

Some men in their thirties, perhaps newly married and with young children, loved gaming in their adolescence but can't justify the time or expense of owning a decent gaming PC.[2] Members of this demographic can drop by PC bangs after work to play the latest games, on the highest-spec PCs, all without spending too much money—or drinking heavily and giving themselves a serious hangover the next day.

One downside to socializing with colleagues at PC bangs, however, is the risk of work hierarchies translating to the leisure environment. While I was working in Korea, my team leader was a pretty good Zerg player. He was also

---

[1] Beloved South Korean spirit that is similar to a diluted vodka.

[2] To be more precise, because it is too costly, or too shiny, or takes up too much space (respect to all the gamer husbands!).

a major "backseat driver." Every time we went to a PC bang on a work evening out, he stood behind us and tried to give us directions. Imagine getting orders at work from your team leader, then receiving more orders at a PC bang while playing *StarCraft*. That was a legit double whammy.

THE UBIQUITY OF ESPORTS IN KOREAN CORPORATE CULTURE

Two decades since the advent of the *StarCraft* boom in the late nineties, competitive gaming is completely integrated into Korean culture. The teenagers and college kids who enjoyed playing games back then have become a central part of Korean society, with decision-making power within their organizations. Yesterday's gamers are now shaping today's culture.

Let me give you an example. After graduation, my first job was with an automotive manufacturer in South Korea.[3] I was one of more than ten thousand engineers at the manufacturer's R & D center, and I naturally felt an element of peer pressure about how I spent my lunch break. Most people hoovered up their lunch as quickly as possible,[4] trying to save as much precious leisure time as possible for hobbies such as working out, practicing golf, playing table tennis, or watching TV.

---

3   I was hired as a senior research engineer at Hyundai Motors Research and Development Center in Namyang, a city in the middle of nowhere.

4   I refuse to call that act "eating" or "chewing."

Some people played games. Only about ten people in our team were up for a round of *StarCraft*, but everybody in the internal network had the software, so arranging a match was a piece of cake. There was time for two short matches or one long match, then lunchtime was over, and it was back to work.

This pattern continued daily, and I soon learned that it was more than simply a pleasurable way of passing a lunch hour. It was a practice session for a serious competition. About twice a year, the center where I worked held a sports tournament to promote inter-team communication and build a healthy community.

Matches took place on a team basis, with handsome prizes for the top three finishers. Winning teams could expect to see their menu at the post-game get-together upgraded from *samgyupsal* to beef or seafood BBQ. Some people took the tournament seriously. For team leaders, it was a pretty big deal.

The punchline? The tournament consisted of several different sports, namely basketball, soccer-tennis,[5] table tennis, and *StarCraft*. Yes, *StarCraft*. By the time I started my first job, *StarCraft* was already part of a leading Korean conglomerate's sports competition.

---

5   This is probably the most popular sport at Korean military bases, also known as *jokgu* in Korean.

Just prior to accepting a job offer and relocating to Korea, I lived in the United States for more than six years. I was astonished to see that even team leaders in their late forties or early fifties—people who seemed unlikely *StarCraft* fans—were good players. They had memorized the keyboard shortcut keys and the unit build orders by heart.

This is what happens when esports becomes an integral part of a country's culture.

HOW TO BEAT A SEMI-PROFESSIONAL PLAYER

During this period, our team contained a semi-professional *StarCraft* player. He was too good. One-on-one, nobody could match him. He beat all challengers within twenty minutes, often ten. He produced too many units, controlled them too perfectly, and had a great understanding of the flow and timing of his opponent. He was invincible.

Despite his superb performance, however, our team never triumphed in the esports tournament at work. I found that quite peculiar, so I watched the next tournament event carefully. This is what I saw. The guy was quite famous within the organization, so every opposing team knew that they couldn't afford to let him take control of the game. *StarCraft* matches were always three-on-three, so opposing players produced attack units as quickly as possible, then sent them all into battle against our star player.

He may have been invincible one-on-one, but he couldn't survive a joint assault from three players. In traditional sports such as soccer or basketball, it's possible to mark a star player with multiple players—an opposing team might try to block Lionel Messi using three defenders, for example—but this leaves open space for other players to use to their advantage. In *StarCraft*, a player whose base has been eliminated is out of the match permanently. The team must continue the battle shorthanded (two-on-three), which is a huge disadvantage.

LIFE AFTER ESPORTS

As described earlier, the professional life of an esports player is a short one. As the esports scene matured, star players moved on to other endeavors, some related to esports and others not.

Lim Yo Hwan (the Roger Federer of esports) transitioned easily into becoming a TV celebrity. He frequently appeared on entertainment shows, sharing his experience of being a legendary esports player. He also married a famous Korean actress, Kim Ka Yeon.[6] Later, he started a second career as a professional poker player, earning a few titles and perhaps more prize money than he ever did as an esports player.

Hong Jin Ho (Mr. Number Two) also became a TV celeb-

---

6   Yes, this pro-gamer got a real actress wife. Can you imagine? No, I'm not writing out of jealousy.

rity. When he appeared on a TV show called *The Genius*—an elimination show designed to test the IQ of participants—he impressed many viewers with his intelligence and ability to make quick decisions. He also appeared on other TV shows and became known primarily as an entertainment talent who used to play games seriously. He topped off this new career with some romantic scandals with beautiful Korean pop singers. Mr. Hong is still active in the entertainment scene.

Guillaume Patry, the handsome French-Canadian player who created many now-standard Protoss build orders, followed a similar path to Mr. Lim and Mr. Hong. He learned to speak Korean and became a main cast member on a TV program called *Non-Summit*, where diverse foreign nationals living in Korea were convened to give a foreigner's perspective on various topics. This increased his fame.[7]

Bertrand Grospellier, the poker-faced French player who always wore shades, is perhaps the wealthiest former esports star player. After the *StarCraft* League concluded, he too became a professional poker player, relocating from Seoul to Las Vegas. With his intelligence and game-savviness, he soon reached the top of the American poker scene, earning prize money that dwarfed the rewards from

---

[7] In a recent interview, he revealed his journey in Korea was not always easy. For example, he was tricked by his manager, which cost him most of his savings. The latest news I've heard is that he quit the entertainment business and returned to his hometown in Canada.

his videogaming days. Under a new alias, ElkY, he has achieved global stardom in the poker scene.[8]

Seo Ji Soo, the beautiful and skillful female professional player, has become the CEO of an online apparel company. She also runs her own YouTube channel, where she still plays good *StarCraft* and tells stories from her professional days.

Kim Ga Eul, the female professional who used to be an engineer, became the coach of the top esports team Samsung Khan. Under her guidance, her team won several championships. Later, she became the director of team Khan. She is the only player in Korean esports history who has won the championship title as a player, a coach, and a director. She is now CEO of her own esports team, called Griffin.

OTHER ESPORTS PLAYERS?

After the scandal in 2010, the South Korean esports market shrunk to the extent that many professional players had to find other ways of earning a living. But that does not mean the overall quality of South Korean players degraded. In multiple games, such as *StarCraft II*, *League of Legends*, *Overwatch*, and *Warcraft III*, the highest-ranked players in the world still came from South Korea.

---

8   No doubt he still reminisces about his *StarCraft* years, as we all reminisce about our elementary school days. He still wears shades at all times, a habit that earns him lots of respect from me.

The big difference between pre-2010 and today's esports scene is that the best players are not confined to domestic teams and leagues. They can go global. Since the rise of the esports industry in countries like the United States and China in the late 2000s, global esports organizations have taken center stage. There are international esports teams based outside of Seoul whose members command high salaries. In 2019, prestigious business magazine *Forbes* released a valuation of the top international esports teams. The value of the number one team, based in LA and London, was estimated at $400 million.

Some teams consist of players from diverse locations. Team Liquid, ranked number three on the *Forbes* list with a value of $320 million, refers to itself as "a multi-regional professional esports organization based in the Netherlands," according to Wikipedia. The team features more than a dozen rosters, including players from all over the globe. The FPS rosters have a strong North and South American presence, while fighting games like *Street Fighter* and *Tekken* are dominated by the Japanese, with the exception of *Smash Bros.*, whose roster is 100 percent American. South Koreans dominate MOBA/RTS rosters, such as *League of Legends* and *StarCraft II*.

For many esports players, being part of a team like Team Liquid, which is owned by an investment group that includes Golden State Warriors co-owner Peter Guber and

NBA Hall of Famer Magic Johnson, is a dream come true. For non-English-speaking nationals, being able to communicate in English has become an essential prerequisite of success.

Are esports professionals happy? It seems so. A comprehensive survey conducted by the Korean government in 2016 showed that 76 percent were satisfied with their income, 86 percent with the social recognition they receive, and 76 percent with their lives overall.[9]

THE GLOBAL ESPORTS MARKET

Korea is no longer the biggest esports market in the world. Other countries, such as China and the United States, have overtaken Korea, at least in terms of sheer size. As the birthplace of video games, the United States has a strong video game industry and is the home of major game publishers such as Blizzard (now Activision Blizzard; the publisher of *StarCraft*, *Overwatch*, and *Warcraft*), Riot Games (*League of Legends*), and Valve Corporation (*Dota 2* and *Counter-Strike*). The esports scene in the United States gained momentum through the popularity of *League of Legends* (also known as LoL) and Twitch, which is now a subsidiary of Amazon.

In China, which has the largest gaming market globally, the

---

[9] A survey of forty-two professional South Korean esports players conducted by Korea Creative Content Agency (KOCCA).

scene is similar to South Korea. *World of Warcraft* (or WoW), another Blizzard production, has been central to the development of the Chinese esports market, as have businesses similar to PC bangs. Technology conglomerate Tencent has taken a central role in developing the esports ecosystem in the country, extending its influence throughout the world after acquiring Riot Games in 2011. Tencent now owns all the copyright and IP related to LoL, the esports game with the largest community in the world.

In Europe, countries such as Sweden, Germany, the United Kingdom, Russia, and Poland have carried the esports torch via games such as *Call of Duty* (another FPS game), *FIFA* (a soccer game), and *StarCraft*. Esports game genres and titles are as diverse as the races and languages of Europe, so it is difficult to tell a single comprehensive story behind the scene's evolution on that continent. We can say that many European countries have fully embraced esports and it continues to grow in popularity.

Not every country has been so enthusiastic. Japan, where I am currently working as an esports consultant, is considered a slow starter in esports business. Nonetheless, it has the third-largest video gaming market in the world, with great potential for the growth of esports. Southeast Asian countries such as Vietnam, Thailand, and Indonesia are also taking esports to their hearts, with growing markets and enthusiastic fans. South American countries such as

Brazil and upcoming global powerhouses such as India are also showing strong esports growth.

It is truly a global scene.

UNIVERSITIES WITH AN ESPORTS CURRICULUM

The once-glorious Air Force team ACE has been consigned to history, but young esports enthusiasts now have other formal channels through which to pursue their passion. Some universities have established a dedicated esports department, providing an esports curriculum focused not only on playing games professionally but also on team management, tournament planning, marketing, and PR.

Yonsei University, one of the most prestigious private research universities in Seoul, announced that it would initiate an esports curriculum, with the help of the Korean government.

NEW BUSINESS OPPORTUNITIES

It should be clear by now that the esports scene has brought many new business opportunities. But it's worth revisiting the question of what makes it different from the traditional videogaming market.

As I mentioned in chapter 1, the key difference between

esports and traditional video gaming is the *audience*. It is fun to watch people play games competitively, and some spectators are willing to pay for this privilege. People enjoy watching professionals duel over *StarCraft* as much as they enjoy watching Netflix dramas and sports matches.

Traditionally, video gaming has been a player-centric B2C market, meaning game publishers and other stakeholders target video game players, who buy hardware, software, and other related products. Esports, on the other hand, is a viewer-centric B2C and B2B2C market. Content and service providers are targeting viewers of competitive gaming through online streaming services, offline tournament events, and sponsorship of teams and tournaments. This is a change of paradigm for the video gaming world.

Because it is aimed at viewers, the esports business ecosystem is remarkably similar to the traditional sports business. Professional esports teams manage a pool of professional players. Those players compete for prizes in tournaments organized by event organizers. Events, teams, and players are sponsored by companies that want to increase awareness of their brand among a specific target audience. Broadcasts of these events are consumed by fans through online streaming services.

One notable difference between esports and traditional sports is the use of video games. As discussed in chapter 8, game publishers must give their permission for their IP to be used commercially. With the exception of fees paid to game publishers, esports business revenues are similar to revenue breakdowns in other sports.

The esports ecosystem has been evolving for twenty years, and it continues to evolve. Where do people go to play games? In some countries, they congregate at PC bangs or net cafes, where they share tricks and tactics, like gym buddies comparing gaining strategies. Where do gamers go in your country or neighborhood?

It's common for people to visit sports bars, where they watch important ball games over a Blue Moon and an order of spicy buffalo wings. The presence of a crowd of other people, all gathered for the same purpose, enhances the experience. In places such as Las Vegas, where there are esports arenas inside casinos, esports fans can gather in a similar fashion to eat, drink, and watch important esports games. These arenas also sell merchandise, such as jerseys. In your culture, where would you go to watch competitive video games?

Traditionally, video games were played on specific game consoles, such as Sony's PlayStation, or on PCs. Now, millions of people play games or watch streaming content on their smartphones and tablets. This can consume lots of mobile data, making venues that offer free Wi-Fi services oases to young mobile gamers who cannot afford—or whose parents won't pay for—expensive unlimited data plans. Where I live, I often see young gamers gathering over Big Macs at a local McDonald's that provides free Wi-Fi services. Do you also see this in your neighborhood?

Technology continues to advance. With the rise of 5G, virtual reality (VR), and augmented reality (AR), esports will surely evolve in tandem. Mobile games such as *Pokemon Go* already provide a tantalizing glimpse of the possibilities. As artificial intelligence becomes more sophisticated, will competitive gaming be restricted to humans? Will we compete against AI, or even watch two powerful AI engines do battle? How about drones? Will we watch competitive drone racing?

This book is coming to an end, but the esports industry is just beginning. There are so many unanswered questions, and so many exciting possibilities.

CONCLUSION

Twenty years since my days of avidly playing *StarCraft* as a junior high schooler, I no longer play any games with the same intensity. But I still watch esports matches occasionally. Not recent tournaments, but good old *StarCraft* Leagues on YouTube. Most of the matches I watch happened at least a decade ago, but they are still very entertaining. I'm not the only one who enjoys a good dose of *StarCraft* nostalgia—some videos have millions of viewers. These are classic matches, selected from the thousands that took place and uploaded.

I have watched most of these matches several times, yet I still find them highly entertaining. Why is that? I don't deliberately watch a match repeatedly, but when I stumble over a classic, it never fails to entertain me. I wonder whether fans of other sports still watch old games? Do Arsenal fans relive the good ole days when Bergkamp and Henry were invincible and the team never lost? In this digital age, those games must be available to stream.

The other day, I had a client meeting with a well-known Chinese game publisher. He is a leading figure in the esports business and a veteran of the same *StarCraft* era as I am. My client described the era that I call the esports renaissance as the esports utopia. In his view, there has been nothing like it since. I was happy to hear that I was not the only one reminiscing about the old days, and also that people of other nationalities could feel the same way. I even felt somewhat vindicated. Hopeless old-timers, aren't we?

THROWING AN ESPORTS EVENT AT WORK

A big part of my job is advising clients to be more serious about the emerging esports market. Since the launch of the esports advisory at my company, I have become curious about how serious my organization is about esports. We have launched the service despite the fact that our core business, as a Big Four auditing firm, seems unrelated to competitive gaming. How far has my organization—a formal work environment at the heart of the financial district in Tokyo—truly embraced the notion of gaming at work?

To find out, I founded an esports club. Right away, more

than thirty people signed up. From this pool, we sent a group of the best gamers to participate in a professional esports tournament event held in Tokyo. All of them were brutally defeated, but we learned something about the gulf between the skilled amateur and the professional.

From these beginnings, we moved on to organizing our own esports tournament. For the first iteration, we played the Capcom classic *Street Fighter II*, a title that was initially released all the way back in 1987. We deliberately chose this title because it was so well known we were sure even some of the company's senior executives must have played it back in the day.

After some discussion, we settled on a format for the tournament. It was our very first, so we wanted to make sure we gave it our best shot. Luckily, the office was already home to a cafe with a projector and Bose speakers. We ordered a PlayStation 4 and the game from Amazon and had them delivered to our office.[1] All was ready. As we finalized the rules and settled on the prizes, we realized that—being an auditing firm—handing out cash would probably cause some internal ripples, so we decided to award goods instead. With opportune timing, we found a retail brand that was selling *Street Fighter*-themed T-shirts.

---

1   It felt pretty good having those games shipped over to an environment packed with hundreds of serious working consultants.

The event took place over two days, one day of qualifying and a finals day for the top sixteen players. We even made posters, based on the original *Street Fighter II* graphics but with employees' faces cropped in instead. An all-employee email was sent out notifying people about the firm's first esports tournament and inviting contenders to sign up. Soon, we had enough applicants to make the event a success.[2]

To create a convivial atmosphere, we ordered some catering and drinks. Around fifty people showed up on the qualifying day, more than half of them purely to watch. To open the event, we held an exhibition match between the head of marketing, who had never played the game before, and a recent college graduate who had joined the firm a few weeks prior, and also had never played the game. The young college grad beat the crap out of the marketing head. This was exactly the outcome we wanted, demonstrating how easily digital natives embrace esports, as opposed to older generations.

The victor was a senior consultant. I had never spoken to him before, but he brought his own *Street Fighter* controller, so I knew he was serious. Hardcore fans have controllers

---

[2] My favorite episode was the message from one of our firm's partners—one of the highest-ranked people in the entire firm—saying that he used to play a lot of *Street Fighter* when he was in high school, and if his schedule permitted, he would like to join in. He showed up to the qualifying day, chose to play as Zangief—a character requiring a lot of skill to use successfully—and beat the crap out of his opponent.

that resemble the ones in the arcades. The next day, we announced the top three places, along with their profile photos and the name of their teams. A few days after that, photos of the event were posted on our company's official Instagram account.

It's fair to say that the esports tournament was a success. A few months later, we held another, this time using a different game. Since then, we have organized esports tournaments every quarter, always using different titles. I discovered that organizing a small but meaningful esports event at work was quite easy. More importantly, I found that an esports event could be an effective way of forming internal communities within a company, enabling more healthy interactions between employees. That was pretty cool.

LEARNING FROM HISTORY

History repeats. So does esports' history.

In this book, I've taken you through the history of esports in South Korea. Before it became a global phenomenon, with flashy gimmicks, multimillion-dollar prizes, international professional teams, and live online streaming watched by millions of people, it started from humble beginnings.

The birth of esports was not the result of a single person's effort but rather a series of serendipitous successes, bolstered by seemingly unrelated factors. An economic crisis. A mega-hit game (*StarCraft*) that perfectly suited the new esports environment. A new type of business (PC bangs) that became part of South Korean culture. A fearless cable channel (OnGameNet) that broadcast esports 24/7 before the term even existed. Professional tournament leagues that became the proving grounds for talented esports players. Corporate sponsors, star players, and casters and commentators who communicated their passion to a growing fan base.

What I have termed the esports renaissance was a period of rapid growth, as the ecosystem embarked on a virtuous cycle. The fan base grew, stakeholders became richer, and the esports market expanded. Sadly, a match-fixing scandal broke that virtuous cycle, sending the South Korean esports industry into a downturn. That was not the end of the story, however. The seeds of esports' popularity had already spread to other countries with larger market potential. Years later, as those seeds bloom into flowers, we may be on the verge of another golden era in esports. Maybe we have already entered one.

MODERN-DAY FATHERHOOD

As I mentioned in the introduction, I have two sons who love their Nintendo Switch. Avid gamers, they play for hours every day, to the point of forgetting their homework.

Sometimes this drives me nuts. I am trying to teach them how to play responsibly. In time, I hope they will learn. So far, I think they are improving slightly.

For a few years, I have been living alone in Tokyo, where I work, while my kids reside in the Japanese countryside. I have only seen them in person every other week. I think they miss me as much as I miss them. The good news is that nowadays most video games are online and multi-platform.[3] I'm able to use video games of a way of connecting with my sons from afar.

Whenever I have time, I can easily turn on the game app in my tablet where I can see whether one of my sons, who is registered as a friend in the context of the game, is online. If so, we can play a quick game together. This takes as little as a few minutes, but it allows us to share an experience. We can even voice chat while playing. What a wonderful communication tool video games have become.

My son's latest interest is *Fortnite*, a battle royale shooter-survival game, similar to the movie *The Hunger Games*. We meet up online, my son through his Nintendo Switch and I through my iPad, and hunt down other players as a team. When I get shot down and am reduced to crawling—which happens quickly because I'm hopelessly bad at the game—

---

[3] Meaning gamers can connect to the same online gaming space through any designated device, such as game consoles, PCs, and smartphones.

my kind son helps me out by making bold moves against opposing players and sparing his healing items so that I can run again. In the context of *Fortnite*, my son is definitely more reliable, arguably more adult, than I am.

How many fathers in the world understand the sensation of taking down virtual opponents by blowing their guts away with a shotgun, or with carefully placed headshots from a sniper rifle, with their son as a trusty ally? Probably not many.

NOW WHAT?

As this book draws to a close, I hope you have come to understand both the history and potential of esports. If you're the parent of a game-loving son or daughter, I hope the stories in these pages have lent some legitimacy to esports in your eyes.

Watching gaming videos can be an educational way to understand both the content of games and the appeal from a spectator's perspective. For those who have never played games before, there are countless tutorial videos available on YouTube. Why not explore games and genres of your choice through watching people play them? Some of the games that I have mentioned in this book, such as *StarCraft*, *League of Legends*, *Fortnite*, and *PUBG*, make a great way into gaming. Try them—you may be surprised how much you enjoy them.

But perhaps the best way of all to understand esports further is to ask around in person. Talk to the members of your family—your sons and daughters—who play games. In this digital age, it will be hard not to find at least one person in your family who is a keen gamer. You may be surprised how their eyes shine the moment you ask them about esports.

I will say this. Under the radar, the esports scene has reached a preeminent place in our culture. To members of the younger generation, whom you may face daily over breakfast, esports is an essential part of their lives. It's a growing industry and a cultural touchstone. You may choose to ignore esports, but if you do you will never follow the rabbit who may lead you to Wonderland. Esports can take you to a cultural wonderland where you can connect with the younger generation like never before, or a business wonderland that offers exciting opportunities. Or both.

Alice decided to follow the rabbit down the rabbit hole that eventually led to Wonderland. If you believe it exists, it is your turn to follow the rabbit. I hope this book has convinced you that there is such a Wonderland and that you may find more than you ever dreamed of there.

REFERENCES

e스포츠, 나를 위한 지식 플러스, 조형근, (주)넥서스, 2017. [Jo Hyeong-geun. *E-sports, Knowledge for the Sake of the Nation*. Nexus, 2017.]

Korean Creative Content Agency. *2018 White Paper on the Korean Games*. 2019.

HOW TO CONTACT THE AUTHOR

The best way to reach me and be professionally involved is via LinkedIn. Search my name on Google or LinkedIn, where you can find my profile, past media articles, and advisory service menu. If you happen to own a LinkedIn account, feel free to connect and send me a direct message.

If you would prefer emailing, you can reach me via demystifyingesports@gmail.com.

We may be at two completely different geographical locations, as I am based in Tokyo, Japan, but given the fact that my current employer has a global network of firms in nearly 150 countries as well as the various video conferencing options, I'm sure there is something we can figure out.

Looking forward to hearing from you.

ACKNOWLEDGMENTS

Roy Tomizawa, if I hadn't met you at that sports business conference in late 2018 and if we hadn't had that drink at that standing bar in Otemachi a few weeks later, I probably wouldn't have this book because I never thought of writing one. You're the one who convinced this reckless consultant who was trying hard to start an esports advisory practice at the time that he had a book in him. And here you go. Very grateful for what you did and thank you for the support along the way.

Although this was a personal, private project, I need to spare my gratitude toward the people that I closely work with.

Masahiro Miyahara, for believing in me and letting me do whatever I needed to and making my daily work life a great joy.

Aki Takahashi, for being patient with my pesky marketing-related questions that had nothing to do with work but greatly shaped this book.

My hardworking, one-and-only esports team (Masafumi Iwata, Cody Greene, Yoshiki Tanaka, Yirui Lu, and Jo Mizusawa), who always think a few steps ahead of me yet still have the appetite to hang out playing games with their boss even during weekends.

Yasuhiro Hayashi, for faithfully listening to my raw ideas and taking them seriously in the early days when you were still with us.

Working with the Scribe Publishing team was a tremendous learning experience: not to mention the impeccable technical and operational professionalism when it comes to publishing, but simply how the team engages with their clients itself was an inspiration to me. You are truly democratizing the business process of book publishing from the side of potential authors and, along with many authors who went through your service, I appreciate what you do.

Hal Clifford, for kindly being the living avatar of the target audience. Rob Petersen, for being the editor of this piece-of-work book of mine. Ellie Cole, for coordinating the A–Z of the publishing process and making my life better.

My childhood gaming friends and former coworkers in South Korea, where I got most of my stories for this book.

My family in Tokushima (Yoko, Tadashi, Megumi, and Yukari), for giving me the mental support whenever I needed it, which helped me shift my mindset in more practical terms ("If your book sells, we can renovate our house big-time.").

Special thanks to Yoko, for being faithful to her feelings toward her semi-game-addict grandchildren that eventually served as the best opening for this book.

My parents (Nam and Jin) in Seoul, who always send the aura of support in silence. All those years of gaming as a child were not wasteful after all, Mom, and maybe that's all I'm trying to do here.

ABOUT THE AUTHOR

DR. BARO HYUN is the founder of an unprecedented esports advisory practice at a Tokyo-based Big Four consulting firm. Dr. Hyun's experience growing up in South Korea, the birthplace of esports business, has been central to his success with the advisory business which has a pool of major clients, including the Japanese government. Dr. Hyun has been teaching esports business at Keio University since 2018, and he has frequently appeared in major media outlets like *The Nikkei*, the world's largest financial newspaper. He was the editorial supervisor for the acclaimed book *A Primer on Esports Business* (まる わかり！eスポーツ・ビジネス) by Nikkei Mook, available in Amazon Japan.

CPSIA information can be obtained
at www.ICGtesting.com
Printed in the USA
LVHW050915031120
670566LV00006B/181/J